JAMAICA

TRAVEL GUIDE 2022

BEST THINGS TO SEE, DO, AND EAT!

TRAVEL
GUIDE

CONTENTS

Introduction to JAMAICA

For many people, Jamaica is the Caribbean's beating heart. Jamaica, the origin of reggae music, the Rastafari movement, and all-inclusive resorts, encapsulates many of the region's most beloved and misunderstood characteristics. Is there a simple solution to the conundrum? Come and establish your own view in the region of sugar cane, coffee, and limestone. Your new ideas will almost certainly be surrounded by cream-colored beaches, surrounded by craggy Blue Mountains, and moored in foamy waterfalls.

Most who travel here don't leave the comforts of their all-inclusive resort; those who do typically don't venture too far outside their immediate area. As the third-largest island of the Caribbean, Jamaica is hard to cover in one trip. Rather, it's best to choose your and vacation preferences first, then make hotel reservations appropriately. The three main tourist areas on the island are westernmost Negril, which is known for its beaches and upscale hotels; northwestern Montego Bay, which is popular with golfers; and northeastern Ocho Rios, which is known for climbing waterfalls like Dunn's River.

Some (but not many) people come to Port Antonio's eastern district to experience world-class surfing at Boston Beach, hiking in the Blue Mountains, and river rafting on the Rio Grande. Sign up for one of the greatest tours in Jamaica if you want to see parts of the island that are rarely visited by tourists.

5
THINGS TO SEE AND DO IN JAMAICA

1. CLIFF JUMP AT RICK'S CAFE

This restaurant and bar overlooking the ocean is a popular place for locals and visitors alike. There are huge cliffs to jump off too. It's about 35 feet to the water, so if the height is too much for you, you can just relax and enjoy the view with a drink.

2. GO ON A RUM TOUR

Rum, made from fermenting and distilling sugarcane, is one of Jamaica's biggest exports. Tour Appleton Estate, which has been producing rum since 1749 (they produce 10 million liters of rum each year). Worthy Park and Hampden Estate are two others to visit while here. Tours cost around 4,500 JMD.

3. HANG OUT TO THE BEACH

Jamaica is rich with soft, powdery beaches. In Montego Bay, head to Doctor's Cave Beach. If you want something more secluded, choose Cornwall Beach. In Negril, Seven Mile Beach has something for everyone. And past the overpriced hub around Margaritaville, you'll find quieter stretches of pristine sand.

4. LOSE YOURSELF IN THE CLOUDS

The Blue and John Crow Mountains National Park lies to the east of the island and covers 41,198 hectares. You can bird watch and hike the Holywell Nature Walks that take you through the cloud forest. A short drive from Kingston, this park can easily be visited in an afternoon. Park entrance is 1,480 JMD.

5. EXPLORE MONTEGO BAY

Montego Bay is the place for tourist bars, international restaurants, and epic parties. The ritzy resorts are mostly in Ironshore, just outside the riotous city of MoBay. Gloucester Ave is like the best of both worlds: a quieter touristic setting with cheap jerk restaurants and hole-in-the-wall bars.

10

OTHER THINGS TO SEE AND DO IN JAMAICA

1. CLIFF JUMP AT RICK'S CAFE

For a unique look at the landscape, head to the Port Antonio area and take a guided trip down the Rio Grande River on a bamboo raft. This is one of the best ways to see the many caves, waterfalls, and crystal springs that are tucked away throughout the island. A three-hour rafting trip costs 15,500 JMD per person with Rio Grande Rafting Tour.

2. GO SNORKELING

On Jamaica's northern coast, you'll find a wide array of sea life. Here you can go snorkeling and see coral, stingrays, lionfish, barracuda, and more. Ocho Rios is another exciting place to snorkel, with plentiful scorpionfish, lettuce sea slugs, and nurse sharks. Guided trips start around 5,000 JMD.

3. EXPLORE THE GREEN GROTTO

The Jamaican countryside is littered with over 1,000 caves. The most well-known are the Green Grotto Caves on the north shore. The caves are composed of limestone, and the green algae that gives the cave its name has been etched into the walls by the tides. You'll travel through a forest of stalactites and stalagmites as you make your way through the cave. When the English invaded Jamaica in the 17th century, Spaniards sought refuge here. The cost of admission is 2,950 JMD per person.

4. TOUR THE SUN VALLEY PLANTATION

Learn about the island's history from the slave trade to the present day at the Sun Valley Plantation in Ocho Rios, as well as what life was like on a plantation farming coffee, bananas, and tropical fruits. It's a fully immersive experience in which you'll meet the owners and the dedicated crew. The trip lasts 90 minutes and includes fruit tastings from the plantation. The fact that this plantation historically utilized slaves for profit is not glossed over in this tour.

5. EXPLORE KINGSTON

Kingston, Jamaica's capital, is a rough-and-tumble environment. It's well worth a day or two's visit. Look for historic landmarks such as Devon House, which was built in the Jamaican Georgian style, which was characteristic of plantation buildings built by colonists during the slave trade. It costs 1,775 JMD to attend, and admission includes your choice of snack or beverage. Also worth seeing are King's House (the Governor-official General's mansion), the Prime Minister's residence, and the Bob Marley Museum. While you're here, check out the Dub Club for some live reggae, the National Gallery of Jamaica, the Coronation Market for some shopping, and Emancipation Park for some relaxation.

6. CLIMB THE DUNN'S RIVER FALLS

These falls, which are located in Ocho Rios, cascade over plateaus 600 feet above the ground. If you're feeling daring, you can climb up them, or simply wander along the river's edge and bathe in one of the many turquoise pools at the base of the falls. The cost of admission is 3,700 JMD. Ziplining is available here for 3,900-4,900 JMD per person if you prefer adrenaline activities.

7. BIRDWATCH AT COCKPIT COUNTRY

Jamaica has 150 resident species of birds, with 29 of those species being endemic to the island. Just southeast of Montego Bay lies Cockpit Country, an area rife with nearly 110 of these species. Keep an eye out for Black-billed Parrots, endangered Jamaican Blackbirds, and Blue Mountain Vireos. The area itself is lush and scenic, with sinkholes of dissolved limestone and lots of rivers.

8. SWIM THE BLUE HOLE

Blue Hole is one of the island's less visited swimming locations. A tour that includes hiking to a tiny waterfall, cliff jumping, a rope swing, swimming in azure lagoons, and plenty of breathtaking views costs 3,000 JMD. You can also enjoy river tubing or bamboo rafting for an additional cost. Just keep in mind that there is no place to put your baggage, so if you don't have access to a car, carry a waterproof bag to keep your items in while you swim.

9. TAKE A DAY TRIP TO PORTLAND

This region is off the beaten path and a welcome respite from the coast's hordes. Peaceful beaches, limitless natural beauty, and friendly folks who aren't hesitant to chat you up await you here. Visit the Blue Lagoon, see Somerset Falls, and eat a lot of jerk chicken in Boston while you're here.

10. VISIT THE BOB MARLEY MUSEUM

Bob Marley, one of Jamaica's most famous artists, is often blaring in the background all around the country. Visit his house on Hope Road in Kingston where he lived and worked between 1975-1981. You'll learn about his life, with glimpses into his recording studio and bedroom. Admission is 3,700 JMD.

JAMAICA TRAVEL COSTS

HOSTEL PRICES – A bed in a 4-6 bed dorm in touristy places like Montego Bay costs about 3,700 JMD per night. They start from 2,000 JMD in places like Port Antonio. A dorm with eight beds or more costs from 2,900 per night. A private room with a shared bathroom costs about 6,500 JMD per night and a room with a private bathroom is around 7,400 JMD. Free Wi-Fi is standard and most hostels also have self-catering facilities.

For those traveling with a tent, there are a few campsites in Jamaica. You can get a pitch for a two-person tent without electricity for as little as 300 JMD per night.

BUDGET HOTEL PRICES – Budget two- and three-star hotels start at 6,000 JMD per night in less touristy areas like Port Antonio but are closer to 8,000 JMD near beach resort areas. Expect basic amenities like free Wi-Fi, TV, and occasionally free breakfast.

Airbnb is available everywhere in Jamaica. For a private room, expect to pay from 5,700 JMD per night, while an entire home/apartment averages closer to 12,000 JMD per night.

Average cost of food – Jamaican cuisine is influenced by a mix of Caribbean, African, and European flavors, owing to the numerous countries that have occupied the island over the years. Seafood and tropical fruits are super common here, and popular dishes include goat curry, patties (a savory turnover), saltfish (dried and salted cod), and dumplings.

A casual lunch at an inexpensive restaurant costs around 700 JMD. You'll find stewed chicken or beef on most menus for about 450 JMD, and jerk chicken is about the same price.

A combo meal at McDonald's costs about 800 JMD while a large pizza costs about 2,200 JMD.

If you want to splash out, a three-course meal at a mid-range restaurant costs around 3,300 JMD with drinks.

Beer is around 400 JMD, as is a latte/cappuccino. Bottled water is closer to 100 JMD.

If you plan on cooking your own food, expect to pay 7,000 JMD per week for groceries. That includes basic staples like pasta, rice, seasonal produce, and some meat or seafood.

BACKPACKING JAMAICA SUGGESTED BUDGETS

If you're backpacking in Jamaica, I recommend setting aside 7,000 JMD every day. This implies you're sleeping in a hostel, preparing all of your meals, limiting your drinking, getting around by bus, and largely doing free activities like lying on the beach and swimming. If you intend to drink, increase your daily budget by 400-1,200 JMD.

On a daily budget of 16,500 JMD, you can stay in an Airbnb, eat out a few times, have a few drinks, take the occasional cab to travel around, and participate in some paid activities such as rafting or snorkeling.

On a "luxury" budget of 30,000 JMD or more per day, you can stay in a hotel, eat out for all your meals, drink more, rent a car to get around, and do whatever tours and activities you want. This is just the ground floor for luxury though. The sky is the limit!

You can use the chart below to get some idea of how much you need to budget daily, depending on your travel style. Keep in mind these are daily averages - some days you spend more, some days you spend less (you might spend less every day). We just want to give you a general idea of how to make your budget. Prices are in JMD.

	ACCOMMO-DATION	FOOD	TRANSPOR-TATION	ATTRAC-TIONS	AVERAGE DAILY COST
BACKPACKER	3,000	1,500	1,000	1,500	7,000
MID-RANGER	6,000	5,000	2,500	3,000	16,500
LUXURY	9,000	11,000	4,000	6,000	30,000

JAMAICA TRAVEL GUIDE: MONEY-SAVING TIPS

Although Jamaica is a holiday destination, there's more to the island than the resorts. Once you step out of the resort bubble, you'll really lower your costs (and experience a more local version of the country). Here are some ways you can save money in Jamaica:

Shop around for tours – If you're going snorkeling, shop around for the best price as equipment and tours can vary widely even along one beach front.

Avoid spring break – If you visit during the American spring break season in March, you'll pay 25% or more for everything (not to mention have to have to deal with all shenanigans those kids cause).

Enjoy nature – Relax on the beach, go for a hike, or take in a sunset. Jamaica's natural beauty is breathtaking and free, so drink it in!

Pay in Jamaican dollars – When possible, pay for anything in Jamaican dollars. You'll often get a better exchange rate.
Look for deals and discounts – Visit Jamaica has a whole section on their website (visitjamaica.com/travel-deals) dedicated to travel discounts, deals, and bundles. Some are meh, but sometimes there are sizeable discounts on hotels.
Shop for souvenirs at supermarkets – If you want to purchase souvenirs like coffee, jerk seasoning, or hot sauce, go to a supermarket like Quality Traders rather than a souvenir kiosk.
Stay with a local – There are a few Couchsurfing hosts in Jamaica so use the app to find free accommodation during your visit. You'll save money and get to connect with a local who can share their insider tips and advice with you.
Bring a water bottle – The tap water here is generally safe to drink so bring a reusable water bottle to save money and reduce your plastic use. LifeStraw is my go-to brand as their bottles have built-in filters to ensure your water is always clean and safe.

WHERE TO STAY IN JAMAICA

Jamaica has a fair number of hostel and budget accommodations around the country. Here are my suggested places to stay:

MOBAY KOTCH (MONTEGO BAY)

FIVE GABLES (MONTEGO BAY)

REGGAE HOSTEL (KINGSTON)

RAGGAMUFFIN HOSTEL &
COFFEE BAR (KINGSTON)

JAY'S GUEST HOUSE (BLUE MOUNTAINS)

HOW TO GET AROUND JAMAICA

PUBLIC TRANSPORTATION – Jamaica has an extensive transportation network of buses and mini-busses that link almost all the villages and towns — and they're ridiculously cheap. There is often no set timetable though so buses leave when they're full. For that reason, make sure you're flexible when taking the bus.

Buses and mini-busses charge around 100-170 JMD.

TAXIS – Taxis have a 200 JMD starting fare and charge 400 JMD per kilometer. While affordable, they add up fast so use them sparingly.

BUS – Coach buses can get you to and from most of Jamaica's touristy destinations. Knutsford Express is one of the most popular buses, with a two-hour trip between Kingston and Ocho Rios costing about 2,300 JMD. A four-hour trip from Kingston to Montego Bay is about 3,400 JMD.

CAR RENTAL – Car rentals can be found for around 5,700 JMD per day for a multi-day rental. Renters need to be 21 and have an International Driving Permit (IDP).

SCOOTER RENTAL – You can rent a scooter or motorcycle from various places around Montego Bay, Negril, and Ocho Rios for about 4,500-7,500 JMD per day, with motorcycles being on the higher end. Remember to always wear a helmet!

BICYCLE – The roads here aren't the safest for cycling, but if you want to rent a bike, expect to pay around 3,000 JMD per day.

HITCHHIKING – Hitchhiking is not common here for tourists as public transportation is super affordable.

WHEN TO GO TO JAMAICA

The weather in Jamaica is pleasant all year, with temperatures ranging from the mid-20s°C (70s°F) to the high-30s°C (high 80s°F).

The peak season for the island is from January to March, when prices skyrocket all over the place. This is the busiest time on the island.

Avoid busy holidays like Christmas, Easter, and Spring Break to avoid crowds. At most resorts and beaches, though, you will be surrounded by tourists. Prices are also significantly higher.

HOW TO STAY SAFE IN JAMAICA

Although Jamaica is a reasonably secure destination to backpack and travel, crime does occur, particularly at night and in the country's party regions. Pickpocketing is a prevalent form of petty theft, so keep a look out. While at the beach, never leave your belongings unattended.

When you're out and about, don't show off your cash or valuables. If at all feasible, keep them in a safe deposit box at your hotel. This is particularly true in popular tourist destinations such as Montego Bay, Ocho Rios, and Negril. Break-ins can happen at any time, thus keep your hotel/doors accommodation's and windows closed at all times.

Kingston is, unfortunately, no stranger to violent crime and gang activity. If you want to explore Kingston, do not go out alone at night and never walk home alone at night if you've been drinking.

LGBTQ travelers should practice caution here. Homophobia is rampant and there are laws against

If you're concerned about being scammed, here's a list of common travel scams to avoid.

Dial 110 for an ambulance or the fire department if you have an emergency. For police, dial 119.

Always go with your gut feeling. At night, stay away from lonely regions and be mindful of your surroundings. Make duplicates of your personal documents, such as your passport and identification, and don't carry too many valuables.

Remember, don't do it in Jamaica if you wouldn't do it at home!
Also, be sure you have adequate travel insurance. You are covered by travel insurance against illness, accident, theft, and cancellations. It provides comprehensive protection in the event that something goes wrong. I never go on a trip without it as I've had to use it many times in the past.

JAMAICA TRAVEL GUIDE: THE BEST BOOKING RESOURCES

These are the firms that I prefer to utilize when I travel. They continuously offer the best discounts, provide world-class customer service and outstanding value, and outperform their competitors in every way. They're the firms I use the most, and I always start my search for travel offers with them.

SKYSCANNER – Skyscanner is my favorite flight search engine. They search small websites and budget airlines that larger search sites tend to miss. They are hands down the number one place to start.

HOSTELWORLD – This is the best hostel accommodation site out there with the largest inventory, best search interface, and widest availability.

BOOKING.COM – The best all around booking site that constantly provides the cheapest and lowest rates. They have the widest selection of budget accommodation. In all my tests, they've always had the cheapest rates out of all the booking websites.

INTREPID TRAVEL – If you want to do group tours, go with Intrepid. They offer good small group tours that use local operators and leave a small environmental footprint. And, as a reader of this site, you'll get exclusive discounts with them too!

GET YOUR GUIDE – Get Your Guide is a huge online marketplace for tours and excursions. They have tons of tour options available in cities all around the world, including everything from cooking classes, walking tours, street art lessons, and more!

SAFETYWING – Safety Wing offers convenient and affordable plans tailored to digital nomads and long-term travelers. They have cheap monthly plans, great customer service, and an easy-to-use claims process that makes it perfect for those on the road.

JAMAICA TRAVEL COSTS

If you're planning a trip and need some advice on what to bring, here are my recommendations for the best travel backpack and what to bring!

THE BEST BACKPACK FOR TRAVELERS

What's the best backpack for traveling long-term? I recommend the REI Flash 45 Pack. It's light and comfy, top loading, and fits perfectly in an airplane's overhead bin.

SIZE: 45-47L

STRAPS: Thick and cushy with compression technology that pulls the pack's load up and inwards so it doesn't feel as heavy.

FEATURES: Removable top lid, pocket at the front, hydration compatible, contoured hip belt.

HOW TO CHOOSE & BUY THE RIGHT TRAVEL BACKPACK

These are the firms that I prefer to utilize when I travel. They continuously offer the best discounts, provide world-class customer service and outstanding value, and outperform their competitors in every way. They're the firms I use the most, and I always start my search for travel offers with them.

These days, there are so many backpacks out there that it can be confusing knowing how to pick the right one.

Knowing what the finest travel bag is — and how to choose one — is actually a science. I spent weeks choosing my first travel backpack when I first started traveling. I tried on several, conducted hours of online research, and put them through their paces in the store to get a sense of how they would perform.

It took a long time to complete. That study, however, paid off, as my first backpack lasted me eight years.

In truth, I only got a new backpack because my old one was lost by an airline. That backpack would still be around today if it hadn't been lost.

There are many places in the world where you can buy a travel bag - and many more places where you can buy one.

JAMAICA TRAVEL TIPS

BEST MONTHS TO VISIT

November through mid-December is the best time to visit Jamaica. That's when the island's already lovely weather (which ranges from the mid-70s to the high-80s all year) is at its best, and hotel and airfare deals are easiest to come by. Summer rates are likewise low, but you'll be exposed to hurricane season's wrath. The main travel season for the island is from January to March, when hotel room rates can reach over $700 per night.

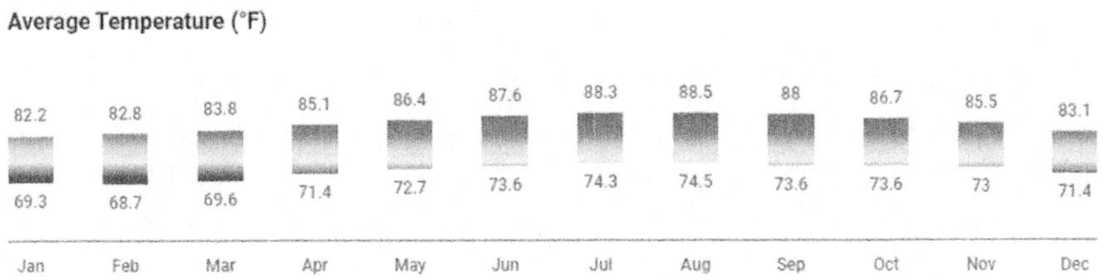

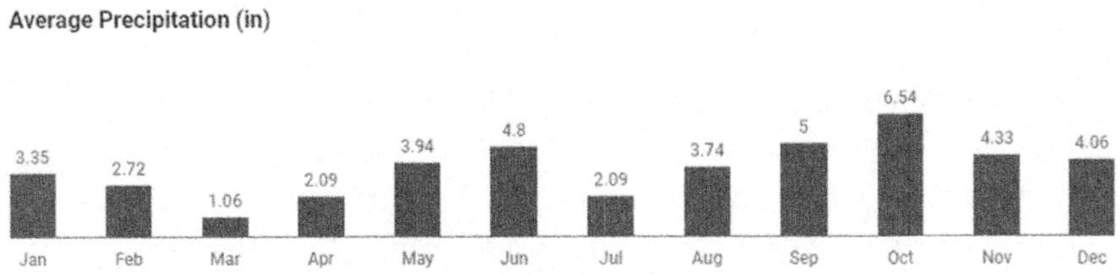

NOVEMBER-DECEMBER

The Caribbean hurricane season ends in late fall and early winter, leaving behind sunny skies and average temperatures of 75 to 85 degrees. Try to book your vacation before the mid-December holidays to obtain the best deal (the danger of rainy season keeps prices low at most of the area's resorts).

Key Events:

Restaurant Week (November)
Junkanoo (All-island, December)

JANUARY-MARCH

Beachgoers flock to Jamaica's shores at this time – particularly in late March for spring break – because the hurricane season is over and the temperatures are idyllic and breezy. But if you want to save some money and avoid crowds, don't plan your vacation for this time of year. If you're intent on visiting during these months, book your accommodations at least two to three months in advance.

Key Events:

Jamaica Jazz & Blues Festival (Montego Bay, January)
Bob Marley Week (Kingston, February)
Bob Marley Birthday Bash (Negril, February)

APRIL-JUNE

Average temperatures rest between the mid-70s and high 80s, but the weather can be a little rainy. Given the mist, the golf courses and beaches are relatively quiet, and hotels offer incentives to visit in spring. Keep in mind that hurricane season technically starts on June 1.

Key Events:

Carnival (All-island, early April)
Ocho Rios Jazz Festival (mid-June)

JULY-OCTOBER

Flights and room rates are at their lowest at this time of year since these months fall within hurricane season (in the past, Jamaica has experienced the brunt of hurricane season in late August and early September). If you choose to travel here during the summer, it's best to buy travel insurance should some inclement weather halt your vacation plans. Because this is Jamaica's tourist low season, many hotels operate with smaller staffs. This slow period is also when many properties complete construction projects. If you don't mind these caveats, you'll be greeted with uncrowded sands, restaurants and golf courses. Pack an umbrella and some rain gear just in case.

Key Events:

Reggae Sumfest (Montego Bay, July)

POPULAR TIMES TO VISIT JAMAICA

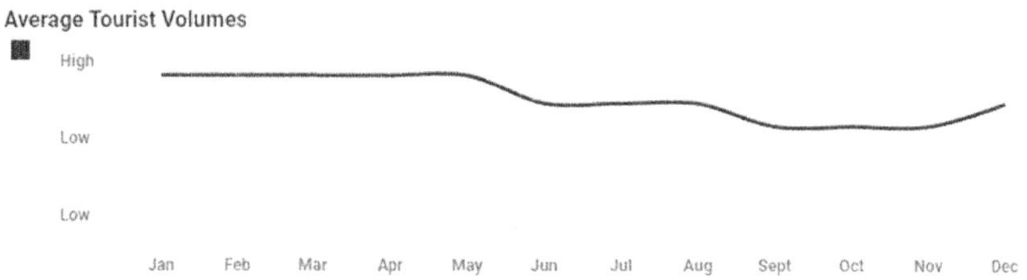

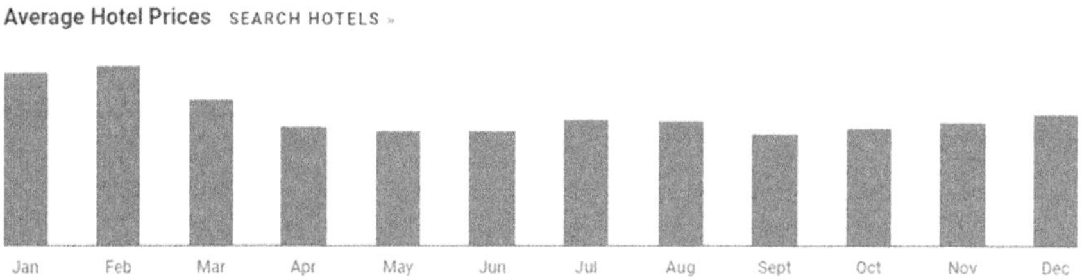

HOW TO SAVE MONEY IN JAMAICA

LEARN TO HAGGLE Bargaining for a better price is expected and encouraged in many souvenir shops. When visiting the craft vendors or taking a cab ride, don't accept the first amount quoted to you.

PAY FOR IT ALL UPFRONT
Jamaica is the nerve center of the all-inclusive. Many of the resorts include more than just food and drinks in their packages

SKIP SPRING BREAK
Throughout March and early April, prices at area resorts skyrocket thanks to an influx of spring break crowds.

WHAT YOU NEED TO KNOW

IT'S THE HOME OF REGGAE

From ska, rock steady and dancehall to anything by Bob Marley, you'll hear a lot of great music wafting through the hotel lobbies and vibrating poolside.

IT'S THE HOME OF JERK SEASONING

This spicy-smoky rub tastes good on many types of meat, fish and even tofu. Try it for yourself and then take a few jars home.

IT'S THE HOME OF JAMES BOND

From his home on the north coast, author Ian Fleming wrote many novels and short stories about the British secret agent.

CULTURE & CUSTOMS

Jamaican culture has often been lumped together with Caribbean culture – though it is true that the music, food and phrases from Jamaican culture have pervaded other nearby islands. But more so than other Caribbean islands, Jamaica's strong ties to its African history play a large role in its modern culture.

Jamaicans speak English, but use a number of idioms that may not easily translate for tourists. In fact, many have been adopted from the Rastafarian religion and culture. For example, when a Jamaican says, "all fruits ripe" it indicates that all is well.

Jamaica's currency is the Jamaican dollar; roughly one U.S. dollar is equal to 133 Jamaican dollars. You can pay in U.S. dollars at most of the island's resorts, especially those that are all-inclusive. When dining out, servers in restaurants usually expect a tip equal to 10 to 15 percent of the bill; if the service charge is already included, travelers can add an additional 3 to 5 percent based on good service. Note that at most all-inclusive resorts, tipping is included in the cost. Don't worry about carrying cash with you at all times; most hotels and restaurants accept credit cards.

WHAT TO EAT

Jamaica is known for unique cuisine that fuses flavors and ingredients from different cultures. Seafood is a staple, and no Jamaican vacation is complete without sampling some of the island's fresh produce or main courses enhanced with some zesty jerk seasoning. Where to dine largely depends on where you're staying, but many area restaurants serve traditional dishes like ackee and saltfish, callaloo (a stew-like soup commonly made with okra and spinach) or fried plantains. To try some spicy jerk seasoning, look for the nearest roadside stand and order a jerk chicken skewer or jerk pork with rice and peas.

Although many travelers choose to dine from the all-inclusive options at their hotels, Jamaica has hundreds of restaurants – some of which are worth venturing off the beaten path for. The beachside Blue Mahoe Restaurant in Negril, attached to The Spa Retreat hotel, earns high marks among travelers for its views (especially at sunset) and diverse menu. Scotchies is an affordable restaurant known for its delicious, local fare in Montego Bay. Meanwhile, Miss T's Kitchen in Ocho Rios serves up a colorful experience and a menu of healthy plates.

BLUE MAHOE RESTAURANT

MISS T'S KITCHEN

SAFETY

It's important to remember that some areas of Jamaica are safer than others. When going at night, employ caution, avoid taking buses, and stay in groups if at all feasible. Because petty theft has been recorded in the past, keep your valuables close to you at all times. According to the United States Department of State, Even at all-inclusive resorts, according to the State Department, violent crime can occur. Violence is notably prevalent in Kingston, Montego Bay, and Spanish Town. For further information, go to the state department's website.

GETTING AROUND JAMAICA

Taxis are the finest method to move around Jamaica, whether you're flying in or out of one of the airports (Montego Bay's Sangster International Airport (MBJ) is the most accessible to the tourist regions). Renting a car is also an option, although driving on the left side of the road can be tricky, with confused road signs, aggressive drivers, and numerous potholes. Many cruise lines visit Jamaica, including Carnival, Celebrity, and Holland America. They usually travel to Montego Bay in the northwest or Ocho Rios in the northeast of the island.

ENTRY & EXIT REQUIREMENTS

All United States citizens will need a passport for entry into and exit out of Jamaica. And keep in mind that customs officials may ask you to provide evidence of sufficient funds for your stay plus evidence of a return trip to the U.S. or an onward journey. A departure tax is generally included in the cost of your airfare; you won't be charged an additional fee upon leaving Jamaica. For more information on entry and exit requirements, visit the U.S. State Department's website.

LOSING YOUR MIND

It's The Only SANE Thing To Do!

Daniel Rechnitzer

EVERYTHING YOU BELIVE ABOUT YOURSELF IS NOT THE TRUTH!

Losing Your Mind, It's The Only Sane Thing To Do

Editorial Team: Eduardo Ramos Ruiz, Dagmar Bauer, Sonja Rechnitzer & Belinda Campbell

Cover Art: Daniel Rechnitzer

ISBN 978-0-9807827-8-3
1st edition, January 2023
Publisher: IntuitionWisdom.com

Table of Contents

About The Author

Daniel Rechnitzer is an Author, Speaker, Trainer and Inventor. He has written two Amazon Best Sellers – "The All Knowing Diary" and "MIND LIES and the Truths That will Set You Free". He has appeared on several documentaries including "Beyond The Secret – The Awakening" and "Beyond Limitations".

If you ask Daniel what he does for a career, he'll tell you with a cheeky grin: "I talk to the Universe for a living". This ability to go beyond the Mind is what Daniel is known for. He has been accessing insights and wisdom from the Universe since 2004 and has helped change lives around the world. The insights received by Daniel from the Universe, form the basis of all training at IntuitionWisdom.com and all of Daniels books and videos.

"When we see ourselves without the filter of our past, we become connected to a shared Genius, a profound reservoir of infinite knowledge and wisdom, that holds the answers to all of our biggest questions" –Daniel Rechnitzer

Daniel and his wife Sonja founded Intuition Wisdom Institute (IWI) in 2008, a global Personal Development Company with the aim of helping others achieve the extraordinary. IWI teaches people how to 'know the unknown' 'heal the unhealable' and 'answer the unanswered'.

IWI conducts Training Courses, Workshops and Events throughout the world and has helped thousands of people to connect to their "Inner Knowing" to transform their lives and others.

In 2022 whilst completing this book, Daniel completed his dream project, an invention called the 'EnlightenMe Machine'. Revealed to Daniel in his meditations, this device generates a high-frequency energy to help us clear the subconscious mind of a lifetime of beliefs, fears and trauma. This book was created to work hand-in-hand with this incredible device.

Both Daniel and Sonja are highly regarded Public Speakers, Motivational Trainers and Media personalities.

Daniel, Sonja live in beautiful Queensland, Australia.

For more go to IntuitionWisdom.com AND www.EnlightenMe.today

Introduction

Welcome to *Losing Your Mind!* I hope you are as excited as I am about this journey! What? You are not sure if I literally mean losing your Mind? Well, I do. But do not fret—it is not quite what you fear it is. It is actually something you have wanted your whole life, but never knew it!

I know losing your Mind has quite the stigma to it. When we hear this phrase, many of us instantly think of being carted off in a straitjacket to a white padded room. We think losing your Mind means to go crazy or insane, and we are pretty confident this will never happen to any of us . . . at least we hope it will not.

Of course, we believe we are sane now, having a very clear idea in our heads of what is crazy and what is sane. But that is the craziest thing of all. Our very definition of sane is, in fact, insanity. We may think we are not crazy, but I am here to tell you that we are all completely NUTS! (No offence intended).

So, when I say, *Losing Your Mind* is the only sane thing to do, I mean it!

You do not think we are crazy, even a little? You, me, humanity as a whole? Not even a tiny bit?

What am I talking about?

I am talking about how we treat ourselves. We are continuously comparing, competing, pushing, striving, neglecting, exhausting, overworking, keeping up with the Joneses, and hurrying our way through life. We are continuously doubting, cursing, loathing, undermining, questioning, belittling, sacrificing, settling, not believing in ourselves and putting ourselves last for others, money, and our goals. We under-sleep, under-hydrate, under-rest, under-nurture, under-support, under-value, under-appreciate and worst of all, under-love ourselves.

I am talking about the insanity of how we see ourselves: as unimportant, overweight, unattractive, not relevant or accomplished, not smart enough. We are full of regrets, jealousy and resentments, and are always needing to be more, because we do not believe who we are is ever good enough or acceptable.

And that is just in our own lives. I will not even start on the insanity of governments, corporations, educational systems, religious institutions, medical establishments, the media and the military.

Let us not forget the insane way we treat our planet. We over-pollute, over-forest, over-fish, over-populate, over-construct, over-consume, over-cement, over-waste, over-need, and overlook the value, beauty and magnificence of nature and life on Earth.

Insanity is everywhere!

Do not misunderstand me—we are all changing, improving, growing and waking up. It is amazing the shifts humanity has undergone in the last thirty to fifty-plus years. Many of us really deserve a pat on the back.

We can change even faster; our health demands that we keep growing, as does the planet. And to do so, we must understand where all this insanity is coming from.

I have noticed a pattern in all this insanity. We OVER-consume on this Earth, always needing and taking more. But in the way we treat ourselves, there is a lot of UNDER: under-nurturing, under-appreciating and under-loving. These OVERS are coming from these UNDERS.

What we neglect within ourselves, we make up for by taking more from all that is around us. The less we give ourselves from ourselves, the bigger the void within, and the more we must attempt to fill this void by taking and consuming more from people, places and things.

So where is this void coming from?

If you go deeper, beyond how we treat ourselves, you will see even more insanity—the insanity of what we see and believe about ourselves. We have

countless beliefs, most of which are hidden from us, trapped throughout our body, from our subconscious to our awareness, but causing havoc nonetheless, mentally, emotionally and physically.

Here is just a tiny snapshot:

- I am not lovable
- I am not interesting
- I am not wanted
- I am not worthy of a great life
- I am not a success
- I am a failure and a fraud
- I should have done better than what I have
- I am not worth looking after
- Money is more important than I am
- I am a nobody
- I am unimportant
- I am not necessary
- I do not matter
- I have failed

And if you think you do not have these beliefs and THOUSANDS more, guess again. These subconscious beliefs control our lives and create our life experiences from inside of us. They dictate our needs, our thoughts, our decisions and our behaviours.

The bottom line is that our insane thoughts, insane behaviours, insane actions are all coming from an insane identity. And that is because our identity is made-up! Made up of everything we have come to believe about ourselves. Be**LIE**fs! Not just truths, but beliefs. And guess what our beliefs are? Completely insane!

We think our beliefs are real, acceptable, helping not hindering and even a true reflection of ourselves, life, love, and the Universe…but they are quite the opposite. We believe things about ourselves that we would swear are completely sane, but they are insane!

I get that this may be a lot to take in right now. Even just hearing that what you have considered to be *you* your whole life may not be true, is a bit much…but believe me when I say your beliefs are the cause of all your suffering, hardship, pain, anger, frustration, suppression, stress, illness, fatigue, aging, stagnation, holding back, being unfulfilled, lack of inspiration and experiencing emptiness instead of experiencing self-love.

The really crazy thing is that we live by thousands of these insane beliefs, and we do not question them for the entirety of our lives.

We have accepted insanity as our sanity, craziness as our normal.

And where does this insanity live? In the Mind.

I hate to say it, but the Mind is not all it is cracked up to be, so it is time to crack it wide open!

The Mind is what is crazy, and it is time to lose it. We were taught that the Mind is the powerhouse in our life, the source of our intelligence—our genius, in fact.

But that is what is so crazy! The Mind is not the source of our greatness; it is the hindrance to it.

It is not the source of genius, inspiration, or the inner guidance system we call intuition. Nor is it the source of the restful, rejuvenating peace that comes from stillness within. These are all faculties beyond the Mind, not from it.

The Mind is the source of the constant noise, insecurity, fear, anger, ambition, doubt, suppression, frustration, needs, wants and virtually every illness known to the human experience. (I address all this in my first book, *The All Knowing Diary*.)

The Mind is a very powerful recorder, however. It has amassed mountainous volumes of recordings from the very beginning of our life. And when we think of the Mind, we think of all the useful things stored in it, such as our education, the books we read, the skills and expertise we have, the important birthdays and dates to remember, and so on.

But that is not the problem. Because on top of all of that useful and useless information is a Mind made up of our every rejection, disappointment, fear, neglect, betrayal, scary experience, failure, mistake, disappointment and regret. It is made up of our every thought, whether positive or negative, and our every belief about life and how we define, level, and classify ourselves.

The Mind is also made up of what I consider to be potentially the most damaging of all: every conclusion we have ever made about ourselves and life. These ideas, beliefs, hurt, pain, wounding, fears and conclusions make up our entire identity—our Mind—and therefore shape our thought processes and our entire reality.

Our reality begins within the Mind, or better said, "as" the Mind. Our very reality is the reality inside our Mind, on both an individual and global level.

This is the lens through which we see and experience life, and it is hiding the Truth about you, life and the Universe.

So instead of experiencing the free-flowing, expansive nature of Truth, we are living out the full contents of our Mind. And it hurts! It is causing us harm in virtually every area of our life, across society and the planet.

Yes, we have many great thoughts in there, wonderful realizations, learnings and understandings. So, let us bring in more of these! Let us heal the carnage, the insanity of the Mind, so we can have a lot less OVERS from having a lot less UNDERS in our life.

How do we achieve this? How do we go about losing our Mind?

I am glad you asked. There is actually a well-known term for losing your Mind, known virtually all around the world. It is a highly respected and revered practice that many believe takes great discipline and many lifetimes to master.

The term for losing your Mind and going beyond it is "EVOLUTION". Enlightenment is another such term. Both mean the same to me.

Evolution is growth and the ultimate in growth is about reaching a point in life without needing beliefs or concepts about everything. In fact, it is about being in life without the need for a self-concept—your current identity, the person you believe you are. But once again your identity is made up of concepts, not Truth. The reason you experience pain, hardship, stress, and illness is simply by believing a concept that was never true in the first place.

This affects every area of life. If your self-concept is off, then so are all your other concepts in life. The quality of your understanding of the Universe and all that surrounds you stems from the quality of your understanding of yourself and your true nature.

This is why our Evolution is so important. But it is easy to dismiss Evolution as too hard, too time-consuming, not a priority, not realistic, and so on. Many of us do not believe it is even possible, or necessary.

That is the amazing thing about life though—so much of what we believe to be true, is not! And so much we refuse to believe to be true, actually is!

We, along with our concepts of life and our reality, get in the way of discovering the real Truth.

We believe we already know what Evolution is and how long it should take. But like many of our concepts, this one is also false. We simply made it up.

Evolution and Enlightenment are about realizations, not about time. Time has nothing to do with our awakening; it, too, is just a concept.

We have many false concepts in life. It is believing they are the Truth that makes life tricky, because we experience what we believe to be true. That is

how powerful our beliefs and concepts are—they literally determine everything we experience in life.

The moment you form a concept about something, is the moment you experience the fullness of that concept, instead of experiencing the fullness of Truth.

What is blocking a quality understanding of ourselves and the Universe? It is the concepts in our Mind! Concepts are limiting. Our current self-concepts do not serve us, but rather hold us back from realizing and experiencing our true greatness.

But we are very attached to our self-concepts. In fact, we are so heavily invested in maintaining our concepts, keeping them alive, and seeing them as real that we spend our lifetime making sure we experience exactly what we believe. Your life now is an exact mirror reflection of everything you have believed to be true about you and life. But what you believe was never the Truth; they are just your be**LIE**fs.

The longer we hold onto our false concepts, the more we continue to live out a false reality. And we all know what that looks like. It is a reality that takes, depletes and destroys what gives life. But we are attached to what life can bring us. We are attached to our needs, desires, wants, ambitions and goals. However, these are not what makes us great; instead, they leave us feeling empty and unfulfilled.

Life is an unveiling of Truth. From one moment to the next, life is asking us to discard what does not work to make room for what does. We are all learning what the Truth is. This is an inescapable process for every human being, no matter one's religion, race, or creed. It unifies every one of us.

Evolution is really an awakening, beyond the Mind's concepts and back to Truth. It is a willingness to see infinity in all things, rather than insist on being right about what we have always believed to be true. Believing you already know the Truth is the biggest obstacle to discovering the Truth.

This journey begins with a willingness to see the infinity within you and let go of your self-concepts and all the other concepts you cling to. As

you allow all these things to drift away, becoming less and less attached, a new level of awareness becomes accessible. It is an inner awareness where you get to perceive yourself as infinitely more than you have ever imagined yourself to be. You recognize your fullness, your wholeness—not any notion of emptiness or neediness.

When you see your fullness, you no longer need to take more from yourself and your surroundings; instead, you are giving of yourself just by the nature of you being full.

Let's look at an example of a common Belief that often gets in the way of us evolving. And let's look at the Truth. Here we go…

***Belief:* It is not safe to look deeply at myself.**

Truth: We desire better, easier, and more exciting lives. We want so much more for ourselves, beyond the everyday struggles and norms. We want to throw out convention and live the extraordinary!

But to achieve this requires extraordinary introspection, looking deep within ourselves at what is working and what is not.

We have been taught that this is threatening, so we avoid it. And when we do desire personal growth, we do it our way. But interestingly, our way is actually keeping the status quo, not deviating from it. We are quite comfortable where we are at—with what we know and who we think we are. It is familiar—and we like that. When our reality is called into question, we immediately defend it, protect it, and do our best to maintain it.

This is where the blockage is. We defend and protect something that we ultimately want changed. But how can this lead to any serious growth? How can you expect the transformation you desire by vigorously holding onto your current reality? The answer is you cannot.

So, it is time to shake up what you believe is true and turn those beliefs inside out and upside down, because that is how you break the mold!

This brings us to our first Truth.

It is necessary to change your current view of reality if you want your current reality to change. It is necessary to be open to larger, more expansive concepts of yourself and of life if you want your life to expand. The more radical the transformation within you, the bigger the transformation in your life.

Realize: "To experience the extraordinary, I must be open to having an extraordinary view of myself."

How was that?

That wasn't painful or scary, was it?

Of course not.

Well, that's how we do things around here, we bring our awareness to what Belief we are still holding onto and we heal it with some Truth.

Are you ready for more?

YES?

I hope so, because I just wrote hundreds of them for you!!

To get you even more ready I have begun this book with some recommendations to help you get the most out of this journey.

Here they are.

My Recommendations

Here are five simple suggestions to help get the most out of this journey.

1. Let the Truth do the Work!

Truth is powerful; it heals, awakens, expands—it takes us from where we are now to where we really want to be. All that is required of you is to just keep reading the Truths, at least a few minutes every day. Try to avoid the need to analyze, judge, or scrutinize; just allow the Truth to do its thing.

After you read a Truth, I suggest giving yourself a short break; just sit with the Truth before reading the next one. This allows the Truth to integrate as deeply as it can go. Integration is essentially the rewiring of the brain through "remembering" Truth. To help with the integration, I have also created the amazing *EnlightenMe Machine*. See Recommendation 5.

You may notice some beliefs are covered more than once—this is done on purpose, to enable you to fully clear all aspects of that belief.

2. Recognize Resistance and Self-Sabotage.

Your Mind is the sum-total of all your beliefs. It is an identity unto itself. Ultimately, it is the you that you have come to believe is the real you—but is not. It wants to exist, but the more you discover deeper Truths about yourself, the faster this Mind dissolves. Since it wants to exist as real, it will want to argue with the Truths presented here, convincing you to stop reading, or leading you to believe that certain Truths do not apply to you.

It will feel very real, very convincing. It is how the Mind keeps you from growing and how it stops you getting what you really want in life. When this happens, simply recognize these feelings as non-truth, laugh at

the Mind, and keep reading anyway! Yes, you might not be able to instantly relate to some beliefs, but just keep reading!

3. Reactions are not Truth.

You might experience some reactions during this process. Please note, your reactions are not showing you Truth; they are showing you where you still believe a non-truth and do not want to let go of it. A reaction shows you what still needs healing. So, if something you read causes a reaction, do not quit! It really means that you are close to a breakthrough. Think of these kinds of reactions as signs you are up to big things!

4. Replace Punishment with Self-Love.

Many of us have been conditioned to tell ourselves off and beat ourselves up when we get something wrong or get off-track. This being in the Mind or void is as much a part of your Evolution as being on-track. It is part of the process. Punishing yourself does not put you back on-track; it keeps you off-track even longer. Instead, give yourself love and support if you have a Mind moment, day, or even week! Know this happens when you are growing fast, so get excited—great things are entering your life.

5. Become Familiar with the EnlightenMe Machine.

I created the *EnlightenMe Machine* to help you integrate the Truths in this book on a much deeper level and clear the countless beliefs you are still holding onto as your identity. It is a device designed to raise your vibrational frequency, to help still the Mind, calm the body, and open you up to rapid growth. Think of it as your buddy, your companion on this journey, should you wish to bring it into your life.

What is vibrational frequency? All of life has a frequency, an energy. Positive thoughts such as love, self-belief, and kindness have a high frequency and make you feel good in your body. Anything born of nature has a high vibrational frequency, including trees, mountains, oceans, animals, and fresh food.

Things coming from the Mind, the void, have a low vibrational frequency and do not make you feel good. Such things include guilt, self-doubt, regret, processed foods, cities, mass media and so on.

Often our state of being can drop into lower or negative vibrational frequencies because of our own blockages and self-sabotage, other people affecting us, and the modern technological world we live in.

When your frequency gets low, the best thing to do is immerse yourself in Truth, whether that is from this book, being in your own spaces, having self-loving thoughts, spending time in nature, or now simply being with the *EnlightenMe Machine.*

Use Your Phone Camera To Open Link

The *EnlightenMe Machine*, which uses no electronics whatsoever, generates a highest frequency energy 100% naturally. Its design came to me in my Truth state (no-Mind space) over several years. It is built to elevate your awareness beyond the Mind connecting you back to your True-Self.

In this heightened intuitive space, you can receive clearer answers from within, and clear the Mind of the thoughts and beliefs built up over years. A clearer Mind and Body helps you manifest better outcomes more clearly and easily. The EnlightenMe Machine will also help you feel stronger and supported on your Evolution journey, whether you are reading Truths, or just sitting, relaxing and resting.

My recommendation is that you read this book at least twice, so if you would like to purchase the *EnlightenMe Machine*, do so before your first reading, so it can arrive in time for your second reading.

Is the *EnlightenMe Machine* essential for your Evolution journey?

NO—only Truth is. It is totally optional; you can think of it as very advanced training wheels, a support to comfort, nurture and empower you on this journey and beyond. You will also find it very helpful in integrating the Truths found in my earlier books, *The All Knowing Diary* and *Mind Lies And The Truths That Will Set You Free.*

For more information about the *EnlightenMe Machine* visit: www.EnlightenMe.today

Ready?

So, let us begin this incredible journey of discovering who and what you truly are. Let us go deeper than you have even dared to go before, overcoming the fears, healing the rejections, letting go of the disappointments, and seeing through the identity you made up for yourself all those years ago.

It is time to see yourself as more than the Mind, to go beyond it. It is time to start "*Losing Your Mind*"—it really is the only sane thing to do!

The Journey Begins

Belief, Truth, and so it goes, going deeper and deeper. Welcome to *Losing Your Mind*!

Belief:

This isn't going to work on me, nothing works on me
Truth: Seeing yourself as complicated doesn't work for you. Seeing yourself as lovable, is all you ever wanted.

Money is more important than my awakening
Enlightenment is realising one's true greatness. A high self-worth creates a high net worth. A low self-worth creates a low net worth.

Truth isn't enough to change my life, I need more
Truth has you awaken to your true power. It's all you ever needed.

I can't do this
You think you need to do things as well as others, but you never realized the way you do things is enough.

This won't work for me
You worry you will fail and be disappointed in yourself, but the bigger fear is you won't even try, and that represents an even bigger disappointment for you.

My beliefs are stuck inside of me
Beliefs are energy that you think belong to you. When you no longer need to identify with them they will disappear.

My beliefs are true

Your beliefs are true, but not about you. They are true of the MIND that's it.

Who I think I am is real!

The Mind believes it's real. But you were never the Mind. You are the observer of all its thoughts, feelings doubts and insecurities.

I am nothing, only small and insignificant

The idea that you need to be more is small and insignificant.

I am not enough the way that I am

How you see yourself now isn't enough.

I am only human

You're pretending to be human to belong. Belonging won't bring you self-love. But seeing your 'Self' as love, will.

I need to see myself as human

This is but one idea of what you can choose to be. It is not the ultimate idea of what you are. Be open to being larger, be open to the true idea that is you. It is the ultimate success, fulfillment and health strategy!

I'm not safe

Thinking you are not good enough makes you unsafe. Seeing you were always what was needed in every moment keeps you safe.

I am not important

Needing to be important is unimportant. Rather see that what you bring to the Earth is absolutely necessary. You are therefore far more than important.

I don't matter here
What you think you have to achieve doesn't matter, but seeing yourself as your best achievement is exactly what matters.

I've made too many mistakes
You have had many realizations in your life. Mistakes are a way to see what works and what does not. The mistake was not realizing this.

I regret all my decisions
You regret not being able to receive everything life has been trying to give you. If life sees you as worthy of receiving, you can see yourself as worthy of receiving.

I'm not as smart as I had hoped I would be
Don't expect yourself to know what others know, that's redundant. Rather believe you can know what nobody else knows. That's what matters.

I must push up against life for it to become better
Life is self organising, you need to stay out of its way, and let it give to you in the gentlest way.

I can't ever get the right answer
There is no right or wrong, just what comes from being self loving and what comes from being without self love.

I have to regret my past
Your past moves you into better situations not lesser situations. Your past was not you but what happens when you ignore what is you.

I always miss great opportunities in my life
Life never misses giving you what you need most. You are the best opportunity in your life, you can't miss being you.

I don't want to be seen as a failure and disappointment
You don't want to fail at giving life your best go. But life's not about giving it your best go, just holding the best idea of yourself.

I have to wait for what I want in life
Waiting is in the Mind, because life is always giving you what you need. Become more aware of what you are receiving instead of what you are wanting.

My failures still haunt me today
You learn more from reliving your victories than your self-rejections. You can't be seen in failure or success, you are not a label or a judgment, you are life! Life requires no labels or judgements, it is infinite.

I'm not smart enough to get life right
Smarts have nothing to do with getting life right. It takes love to get life right. Follow what you love most.

Life never works out
A life lived pursuing the wants and needs of the Mind doesn't work out. A life pursuing the wants and needs of the heart always works out.

Life is full of disappointments
It is disappointing to not believe in yourself, to reject yourself and punish yourself. Start being kind to yourself and you will stop experiencing disappointments.

Life will never get better for me
If you want a better life you have to be better to yourself. Being Self-Loving is the better life you have been looking for.

I keep creating misery for myself
You keep taking things away from yourself, so it's time to start bringing in more for yourself. Learning these Truths is a great way to bring more into your life. Well Done, it's begun!

I'm not good at making a good life for myself
What others told you makes a good life makes for not a good life. Come back to a simple life without so many needs and you'll have a better than good life.

I don't make any difference
You being here is all the difference that is required of you. Nothing more is needed from you. Just be you.

I am helpless
Believing you need to be more to do more, makes you feel helpless. Being you is enough and has always been enough.

I don't know what I should want in life
The most important thing to want in life is YOU. Needing anything else is just delayed gratification.

Nothing makes me happy anymore
You have realized that looking for happiness outside yourself doesn't work, but seeing what makes you lovable does.

People always disappoint me
Giving your power over to others and putting yourself last will always disappoint you. See that you have what it takes to create the life you want, not anyone else.

Nothing is good enough for me

You think you are not good enough for you. But you can't do any better while you expect yourself do things and achieve things you're not meant to do or achieve.

I can't get life right

Trying to get life right the way society gets life right, is actually getting life wrong. Come back to the life you really want for yourself not the life that leaves you feeling empty.

I can't get anything right

Judging ourselves for making mistakes is not getting things right. But believing in ourselves is the way to get things right, so start there, because that's the only thing missing.

People don't respect me

Needing others to respect you, is you not respecting yourself. What you seek most is actually for you to respect yourself.

People don't admire me

You don't admire yourself. Looking for admiration outside of yourself is a poor substitute for discovering your own admiration for yourself. Spend time looking at what's admirable about you rather than what's admirable about others.

I am worthless

Looking at everything you are not, everything you haven't done and everything you don't have will leave you feeling worthless. Rather stop looking at where you think you should be, and see all that you have become, all that you know, all that you have seen and all that you have realized, then you will feel full of worth.

I am without a purpose on this planet

Nothing in life is without purpose. You will find your purpose is the breakthrough in your greatest struggle, it's in your deepest realizations, in what you seek most to understand and share in this life.

Life is too hard for me

Your way of life is too hard for you. Stop putting pressure on yourself to do the impossible. Rather, do what is possible and easily achievable. Then you will feel successful.

I can't succeed at what I want

You can't succeed at seeing yourself as the person you think you need to be. This was never who you are. Rather stop trying to see yourself as a person, period. You are more.

I can't have what I truly want

Many of your wants are coming from believing you are not enough and so you need more. What you want most is to see yourself as enough. When you see yourself as enough you will need less and you can't help but have more.

Everyone is destroying this planet

Many people are saving the planet. Many people are destroying themselves. Those that have self-love help the planet those with self-hate ruin the planet. Don't hate those with self-hate it's what put them in that situation in the first place.

I am helpless to make a difference

Don't think how can I make a difference to others and the world but start with how can I make a difference to myself? This is easily achieved, you are doing it right now, and it's what the world needs most.

I can't turn things around

Life is always giving you opportunities to create anew. But believing you are not worth more keeps getting in the way. Life will help turn things around when you see just how valuable you are here.

I'm a disappointment

Reflecting on how many times you have been unkind to yourself is definitely disappointing. But you are not the unkindness. You are the love you always wanted to give yourself, and that's the opposite of disappointing.

I suck

What has sucked is trying to live your life as an "I". Being an I sucks because it was never who you are in the first place. Learning to see you are far more than you mistakenly believed you are makes life great again.

I have to criticize myself

We think criticising ourselves makes us smarter, but it just deters us from ever doing anything really great. Criticising ourselves sends us backward, praising ourselves encourages us forward.

I have to take things away from myself to be safe

We believe if we take things from ourselves then others can't take things away from us. Yet our biggest fear in life is what will I take away next. Safety in life comes from giving more to ourselves not taking more away.

I have to be more like others to be happy

Being less like others makes you happy, but being more like yourself makes you more ecstatic. It's believing we need to be more like others that made us unhappy in the first place.

I have to yell at myself when I do something wrong

We were taught to yell at ourselves by our parents and teachers yelling at us when we were young. It doesn't have us grow as we believe, rather it has us shrink. Give yourself praise for giving it a go, it works much better than yelling.

I'm no good at anything

See that there is no need to be good at the things you think you should be good at. Seeing what you are good at is one of the only things that you need to be good at.

I always get decisions wrong

Trying to be good at making good decisions is like trying to go to sleep. Making good decisions comes from allowing the right decision to reveal itself in time. Good decisions are like plants that need to grow and flower.

I always make the worst decisions

The worst decision you ever made was believing you are your identity. You've been trying to come back from that ever since. Deciding to be less the Mind-Self and more your True-Self is a great decision, one you can be proud of.

I am not loved

You feel unloved because you withhold love from yourself. You expect others to give you love instead of giving yourself love but this doesn't help. The love inside of you, is you. Love is the being you are. Love that you are: Love-being.

I can't not love myself for all I have done

The most painful thing we have ever done is take away who we really are and believe we are the I instead. Remembering you are more than the I is something you can easily love yourself for.

I keep making more mistakes
You keep learning in life but you keep labelling things as a mistake, that's the only real mistake you keep making. It would be triumphant if you no longer needed to label things as a success or failure.

I'm not living the life I always wanted
This is because life is trying to give you much more than you ever wanted. Your wants are getting in the way of something much better knocking at your door.

I can't do anymore
We often burn ourselves out trying to achieve, accomplish and earn more money, and we think this is too much. But what we can't do anymore, is keep trying to prove ourselves. There was never a self to prove, that's why it's so exhausting.

I'm not ok
This belief originates from not being happy with the I we have chosen. We do not feel our I is ok. The I is ok if you stop believing it is you.

I have had enough
It's difficult living out our belief system. Its tiring and painful. It's not life you have had enough of, it's seeing yourself as separate from life that you have had enough of. You are not just alive, you are life itself.

I don't want to be here anymore
It's not life that you want to get away from it's not wanting yourself, that you are trying to get away from. Rejecting yourself won't make you thrive, but seeing what makes you special will.

Life is a struggle
Trying to be more important makes life a struggle. Needing things to be important, trying to get to being more important creates struggle. Know that 'important' doesn't come close to describing your enormous significance.

Nobody cares about me
Do you not care about yourself, but expect others to make up the deficit? The whole universe cares about you, that's why you are here. Care that the Universe cares, and you will feel cared for.

I don't matter here
Thinking you need to matter is the Mind trying to matter, which doesn't matter. Recognising that you are a Love-being is what matters most. Trying to BE anything else never mattered.

I'm not important to others
What's more important than being important to others is being important to yourself. Needing to be important to others won't have you feel important to yourself, just less important.

I'm not worth much
How do you asses your value? Is it based on your income, what you know or how much love you have in your heart. The irony is, those with the most love to give, are those making the biggest difference on this Earth.

My opinion doesn't count
Opinions don't count, only your truth counts. Speak your truth, most importantly listen to your own truth, and trust in your truth, and you will feel that you really do count.

Nobody listens to me
You don't listen to you. How do you expect others to listen to you when you don't? Listen for your greatness in what you say. You listening is far more important than others listening.

I'm not like everyone else
About time you realized it. You're not meant to be. Everyone is a unique idea of the Universe. Tapping into what idea you are is called discovering your life purpose. Success comes from being your unique idea, not anybody else's.

I need to quit before I do more damage
Many of us believe "I ruin everything' but the truth is you make things better on this planet. See that you are already enough, it's trying to be more that creates the damage.

I have ruined my life
Everything in life is an opportunity to grow and receive. Why are you refusing to receive right now? Receiving your greatness is what moves mountains on this Earth.

I have hurt too many people
You have been hurt. You were taught this is the way in life. Stop hurting yourself and you will stop hurting others. See that you didn't deserve to be hurt in the past and you don't deserve to keep hurting yourself into the future.

I don't belong here
You are meant to be here. But belonging isn't necessary, shinning is. Shinning is better than belonging. You are existence, shining its light. That's far better than the need to belong.

I am hated

You carry hatred for yourself, so you feel hated. The hatred you carry is about the I, not you. The I is made-up therefore so is the hatred. Neither are real, but your light is. You are not what is hated but that which is observing the hating.

I am despised

The I despises itself. You are separate from such thought. The more you see yourself as your thoughts the more you feel them as your-self. Thoughts are not you. I am despised, is the I talking.

I am unwanted

You feel unwanted because you reject yourself. But what you call yourself was never your-self, it was the self-belonging to the I. You associated with the thought idea of being unwanted, but what was unwanted was the belief "I am unwanted", it was never about you.

I'm not worth loving

The I is hard to love because it is full of everything we are not. It is a void not a wholeness. What is worth loving is you are waking up to the idea you are not the void of the I, but something greater, infinite in fact.

I have betrayed myself

Our worst betrayal was believing we are the Mind and everything it represents. But the betrayal was the Mind convincing you, that it is you. The Mind betrayed you; you didn't betray yourself. You've been trying to get back to the real you ever since.

I keep giving myself what I don't want

You feel the void of the Mind inside and you try to fill it. Providing for the Mind will never work because its insatiable and not the real you. The more

you give it the more unhappy you will be. Don't give to the Mind, its needs are not your needs.

I'm an idiot

You believe you are an idiot for believing all the horrible things others said about you as a child. Believing in other people's ways instead of your own truth makes you feel idiotic. Start listening to your own inner direction, your own innate intelligence and you'll stop feeling like an idiot.

I'm a loser

We've been calling ourselves horrible things all our life. But we lost out big when we convinced ourselves we need to follow the ways of others. We will fail at this, but succeed immensely in being ourselves. It's a losing strategy to mimic others, because we are losing out on being ourselves.

I can't fix my life, it's too late

While you are still alive its never too late. To fix your life, you must fix how you see yourself. The I can't fix your life it just creates the past over and over again. See yourself as more than the I, as everything you are in life, and life will rapidly transform for you.

I have wasted my whole life

Spending a lifetime seeing yourself as the I will have you feel you have wasted your life. But if you have had fleeting moments of seeing your greatness, nothing has been wasted. The more greatness you see in yourself the more you are fulling your purpose for being here.

I keep making bigger mistakes

We reach a point where trying to give into the needs of the I leads to bigger problems in our life. But it is not you making the mistakes it is the I. Leaving it in control of your life is the mistake. Let love drive the decision making not the I.

I'm not good to myself

The Mind isn't good to you. It takes more than it gives, and promises more than it delivers, that its nature as a void. Seeing yourself as the thoughts the Mind has, is not good to yourself. You are not the substance of thoughts, but something greater. The Mind has thoughts, it is made up of thoughts you are not.

I'm not worth looking after

You have much to give to this world, but it begins with giving to yourself first. Realize "I need what I have to give to myself". Give yourself what you need and you'll stop feeling neglected.

I can't exist as me

Being is You, thinking is the Mind. In the absence of thinking you find the real you. Existence is you. But you can't be you while you see yourself as the Mind. Be, don't think and you will be you every time.

I'm unhealthy

You have unhealthy thoughts about yourself that lead to unhealthy habits. Stop tearing shreds of yourself and you'll stop needing to replace them with innutritious food. A healthy body comes from realizing you are worth looking after. If you are not worth looking after who is?

I'm bad because I'm not in shape

Not every body has to be in peak athletic condition. The Mind strives for perfection yet the stress the Mind places on the body is far worse than an out-of-shape body. Strive for peace within sooner than a perfect body. It's the healthier alternative.

I am a dismal failure

The failure in your life comes from comparing yourself to others and to some imaginary goal you believe you were meant to achieve. You made up

your goals, they were never necessary in the first place. You failed to love yourself despite achieving your goals, that's what has you feel like a failure.

Life doesn't work for me

You don't see yourself as life. You believe you are the contents of the Mind; this is what doesn't work for you. You think you are its needs; this also does not work for you. Be life, rather than be the Mind. It's what your True-self IS.

Life takes what it gives

The Mind takes away. Life is always giving, from the fruits in the trees, the vegetables in the garden, the oxygen you breathe to the realizations that wake you at 3am. The more you see how much life gives the less the Mind gets to take away.

Life doesn't like me

Life loves you, that's how come you are here. You don't like you so you experience life not liking you. What you don't like about you is you forgot how much life loves you.

I lose everything

The Mind destroys what has not come from the Mind, nature loving relationships, the body and so on. It doesn't like what is real because it is not real. We lost everything when we decided "I am". Lose the idea that "I am" and you'll keep more of what's real in your life.

I have to have more to see myself as more

What stops you seeing yourself as more is believing you are meant to have what others have. Find what makes you different to others, this is your magnificence not your weakness. To see yourself as more you have to be open to showing yourself all the more that's already within you. Be open to seeing everything you already are.

I am under threat

Your ideas about what life should look like are threatening. Find the most peaceful version of how life can look, and you'll cease being under threat.

My Mind Is The Source Of My Intelligence

Since a young age we've been taught to nurture the Mind, teach it new things, keep trying to be smarter. Where has that gotten us? Do you feel smart enough yet? Or do you keep feeling everyone else still knows more than you, and you failing to keep up. The Truth is because you already feel "I am not smart enough" no amount of learning will ever change that. Realise, the Mind is not the source of your intelligence but rather the source of your insecurity. Knowing this is knowing enough!

Other people have much more to give than I have

If you see others being more successful than you it's only because they have figured out just how much they have to give. They did that not by focusing on what you or anyone else has but by focusing on what they have. So, stop looking at what others have start focussing on what you have. If you gave yourself the same attention as you give to others, you might be as successful as they are.

I always make the wrong decisions

This comes from when you focus on the outcome you want rather than the feeling you seek you. Feel now what you hope to feel in the future from getting the result you want. If you are making a decision to feel successful, feel successful first. How you come into a decision is how you will feel at the end of it.

Belief I'll get into trouble the more successful I become

you fear rejection from others if you achieve success because you reject yourself now because you think it helps to make friends. Diminishing

yourself makes friends with others who do the same but it's the fastest way to create an enemy out of yourself.

The more I have in life the more people will hate me
The more you see how much you are right now the less you will hate yourself. Take stock of your greatness now, and it will multiply.

I'm afraid I will fail and whatever I attempt to do
You rob yourself of opportunities, this is what you fear. Love yourself for everything you have received in this life and all that you have given to yourself. You will see overlooking this was the only failure.

I am not capable of an easy life
You no longer need to prove your worth to everyone. Your worth is found in how much love you have, that's the most valuable commodity on Earth right now. Loves makes the world go round, not money.

I need to please and impress others
Pleasing others will not bring Self Love. Self love comes from pleasing yourself first. Self love is what you really seek.

There must be a higher power out there somewhere
The power that you see all around is not separate from you but within you. It is you, has always been you. You are this higher power.

Happy outcomes create my happiness
Yes, they can. However, outcomes where never necessary for happiness but the absence of needing them is. You don't need the outcomes you always thought you needed.

I need to create more success in my life
You are hoping to create more success so you can see yourself as a success. Successful outcomes only get created by those who see themselves as a success first. You are allowed to see where you are already truly successful, now.

I am not enough
You were before you needed to compare yourself to others. You were more before you decided you need to be just like everyone else. Love that you never needed to be and where never meant to be anything like anyone else.

I should be more than what I am
You are striving to be different to how you imagine yourself. The truth is you are already different to how you imagine yourself. Don't need to be different, be glad you already are.

I hold myself back in life
You don't need to be on our own back about moving forward, you need to get off our own back. It's being on our own back that creates procrastination. Give yourself permission to do what you love, how you love to do it.

I need love from others
You believe if others love you than you can love yourself. You can't receive self love from outside yourself, but you can realise, self love has no prerequisites. You can love yourself without needing to get everything right first.

I should know more than I know, I should be smarter
Don't fill your Mind with what everyone else knows. An empty Mind is a still Mind. Only in stillness can you know all that the universe knows. You didn't need to know more, just less.

There's something wrong with me
The only thing you are missing is seeing how much you can love. The fact that you have love, that you can love, means there's nothing wrong with you, and there never was. You can love yourself, for that.

I have failed in life
You believe you should have achieved more. But it's ok to fail at achieving what you think you should have achieved because it's what you were never have meant to achieve in the first place. What others achieved was not meant for you to achieve. Achieving was never meant to be achieved. Realizing that is your biggest achievement!

I have not achieved as much as others have
You need to asses yourself to know your place next to others. You want to be seen the way you see them, as important. But what's more important is to see you were not meant to be like anyone else. It's the Mind that's like everyone else's Mind.

I should be doing more with my life
You need to put less pressure on yourself to be doing as much as others are doing. A common misunderstanding that when we Do more, we will Have more and get to feel and Be more. Rather practice Be Do Have. When you are Be-ing more, you'll have to Do less, to Have more! Life was never about doing more but seeing yourself as more.

I'm not allowed to accept myself as ok
It's not common place in society to accept oneself. So, we all reject ourselves as a way of fitting in and belonging. The truth is, it wasn't belonging you seek most, it's being ok to be separate. It's ok to accept yourself not needing to belong.

I feel unacknowledged by others

When you are around people imagining how they see you, you take energy away from yourself. You neglecting to acknowledge yourself is what has you feel unacknowledged. You can look at yourself and all that you have created in this lifetime.

I feel I'm getting behind in life

You often feel you must keep up with the "Joneses" e.g. Earn more, do more, socialise as they do, invest as they do, live life as they do, more yoga, more meditation and so on. But enjoying life more doesn't come from doing more, but loving you the way you are more. If you love yourself more, you'll need to do less to be happier with yourself.

I'm not as good as others at planning for the future

You feel you need to get ahead in life. That's because you believe you have already failed to make smart choices in life. Being clever is realizing that you are still making good choices in life. The irony is, creating a great future actually takes seeing all the good choices you've already made in life, rather than worrying about the choices you've yet to make.

I get everything wrong

We often worry we will make bad decisions and get life wrong. But the biggest mistake we can make in life is not in what we decide but in not recognizing ourselves correctly. How we see ourselves determines what kind of decisions we make, and the outcomes they create. To go through your whole life seeing yourself as not enough will create outcomes you feel are not enough. You can't get decisions wrong, just the space from which decisions are made. Focus on your space, not on the outcome you want or fear you'll get. You never needed to doubt yourself to get life right, just to believe in yourself for everything to work our perfectly.

Life is meant to be difficult

Living through the Mind makes life difficult. What we do to our life is try to be human. Living the way society chooses to live is what makes life difficult. The less you try to live as other human beings the less difficult life will be. Follow what brings you joy rather than following what everyone else does to their life. You are free to live according to what brings "me" the most joy.

I need to do everything right to be a lovable human being.

Let's remove the non-truth from this sentence. There is no doing in our being, and because we are everything, there is no need to get things right because we are already what's right. To love requires no doing, no prerequisites. To be, requires no doing. When you look at who we really are and what we are really made of it is: Love, being, Everything... Otherwise stated we are an "everything, love being. You are Love Being Everything. What's more perfect than that?

I want what everyone else has

What you really want is the experience of not needing what everyone else needs to have. You crave being free from such needs. You crave to be whole within yourself to only need yourself, to be content with yourself. So, the next time you feel envious about what another has, realise you just crave needing yourself. When you give yourself self love, what is there left to crave?

Success happens slowly

This belief blocks your success. We were taught to take in life in bite-size pieces for it to be safe. But abundance is much safer happening in large quantities, that way you recognize it straight away and allow more of it to come in. You are safer in an Abundance of Abundance. That's how the Universe does it.

I worry what people will say or think of me if I allow in big success

One of our biggest fears, is what will we say and think about ourself if others misjudge us for our success. But it's what you say now that is more worrisome. You say: "I must slow down all my success, so people don't see me as untrustworthy and unlikeable. I want people to see me as likeable so I know I can like myself." That you keep saying this to yourself is the cause of your worry in the first place. You will like yourself a whole lot more when you stop saying and thinking this. Realize, you don't need people to say anything about you.

I need to make a lot of money or I'll have a poor life

It's the 'need' to have a lot of money that results in a poor quality of life. To love your life without such a need will give you a great quality life. It's the 'need' that both robs us of a great quality of life, blocks more money flowing in and stops you from seeing how much you already have. The truth is, it's not having more that gives a better quality of life it's needing less. More money isn't the 'more' you have been searching for, it's seeing more in you, that will give you what you truly want, including more money.

If I don't keep needing more money I'll never have more

You think it's wanting and needing that creates more on Earth for you. You worry that without the 'want' you'll see yourself as lazy, unsuccessful, that you're not even trying. But what you are avoiding is seeing yourself as enough. And by avoiding it you create a void within that you believe money will fill. Money won't fill the void, self love will. A lack of money didn't create the void in the first place. You want to fill yourself up, and the way to do that is to know you don't need what everyone else needs. You are free to need less than everyone else. It's what makes you free.

I don't have a great memory and forget a lot of things

Society believes the more you remember the smarter you are. But much of what you want to achieve in life requires more forgetting then remembering.

It's ok to have a lesser memory because it means you are dragging around less of your past, having you be more open to the present and the inspiration within. Be grateful your memory is less than ideal, because as far as memories go, less is ideal. A great memory is not the secret to success, though recognizing the truth in each moment is. You don't need to remember yourself, but keep forgetting what you used to think about yourself". Ask yourself "who am I BEING right now?" It's one of the only things truly worth remembering.

I am afraid to be a nothing and a nobody
We believe the busier we are the more we are achieving in life. This is the opposite, in truth. Go beyond Mind achievement into achievement in your awareness. You're making yourself into a nothing and nobody by replacing yourself with the Mind, and what the Mind thinks is good. The Mind is already a nothing and a nobody, but you are everything!

I can't see myself as enough
We believe people need and expect more from us than you can possibly give. What makes you enough is you seeing yourself as enough. The way to do that is to realise, you can do, and be everything that is required of you this lifetime. You are all you ever needed for a great life, nothing more, nothing less. Believe it.

I don't want myself
Many of us have felt unwanted by others in our life. We decided we didn't want to be this unwanted person, so we chose to not want ourselves. That's when we really became unwanted. You decided, nobody wants to be unwanted, so I don't want to be that person. What you didn't realise in that moment was that you actually weren't unwanted as you originally thought. So you didn't need to not want yourself. You didn't know you were wanted, then and now, so you can forgive yourself for not wanting yourself.

The more I do the more I'll succeed in life

To focus on doing more leads to having less in life. Try focussing on what you love in you, in life, and you can't help but create more for yourself. Life was born from love, so you want your life born from love not the need to do more. You are the more you have been searching for in life. You are what there is to love most about your life.

I need to get the lesson from making a mistake

Many of us punish ourselves so badly for making a mistake that we fear trying anything again. Of course, wanting to punish yourself to get the lesson is not coming from self- love. All lessons no matter their nature, are coming back to ONE massive lesson in life - you deserve to love yourself and put yourself first. If you got this lesson, you've gotten all the lessons.

I've done the wrong thing

Sometimes we slip up and do things we are not proud of. But what's worse than what we did is how badly we punish ourselves for it. The wrong thing is always to punish ourselves for anything we do; the right thing is to apologize to ourselves for ever thinking we deserved punishment.

I need to feel bad for what I've done

Our parents taught us to feel bad for the 'bad' things we did. It was their way of trying to correct our behavior. But what they taught us was to always feel bad if we do something wrong. But no one helped us correct this behavior. The irony is, your worst behavior is making yourself feel bad. Realize it's absurd to think that you deserve to feel bad for learning, for discovering something you didn't know yet. You should feel good not bad.

I've been bad

It got very confusing as a child understanding what learning is - a mistake and deserves punishment versus what learning is - good and deserves praise. In truth all learning deserves praise, it's learning after all. Where this

belief originates from is you judged yourself as bad for judging yourself as bad. Just because there are "bad" ways to learn something, doesn't make you bad.

I have to undermine myself so I am loved

Many of us believe if you stand too tall in life, others will dislike us and cut us down. So, we find ways to shrink, to be small, handicaps like illness, drama, accidents or being slow to learn. We believe if we are perfect, we won't receive love. But if you see yourself as perfect that's all the love you have ever needed. It's our love we needed this whole time, not everyone else's.

I need to do everything the hard way

We often feel guilty if life and success comes easily to us. So we make things harder than they need to be to avoid the guilt. We believe the harder we work the greater the satisfaction. But satisfaction is not a product of how hard we work but how much you love what you are doing. Realize, you can love what you are doing without feeling guilty, so there is no point making life hard for yourself any longer. Making life hard for yourself makes you feel even more guilty.

I'm never going to get it right whatever I do

We often think everyone else is smarter than us, that others would do a better job than how we do things. The people you think would do a better job than you would fail dismally at being you, ending up with a lot less than what you have. Know, when you are more willing to be you rather than thinking about what others would do and how they would do it, your life will work out so much better than you could imagine. You don't have to be like others to be great, just more willing to like yourself and how you do things.

There's more I need to do be a success

Do you think others are judging you? Do you still need others to recognize your brilliance? Or do you still need to show yourself you can be smart in life too? The belief here is actually "I am not very smart" and "I make the wrong choices in life". The truth is seeing you don't need to do anymore to be worthwhile or great is really smart. Know, you don't need to prove yourself to anyone anymore. You succeeded when you were born, nothing else is expected of you.

To be successful I need to know what everybody else knows

Many of us believe we are missing intelligence, and we decided on the objective that we need to be as knowledgeable as everyone else. We believe that unless we read all the books, read all the articles, we will fail at our objective. It's the objective that created the issue not having learned or read enough. Needing to know more than others was never the truth, knowing ourselves is what creates success.

I need to be the best to succeed

At school we were taught only the best will do, only the best succeed in life. So now you believe "I need to be the best or I'll fail". The best isn't required, trusting that what we are is enough, is what's required. You can be great rather than the best and that's nowhere near failing. You never needed to be the best to succeed in life, just be yourself. You are naturally great when you're not trying to be better.

If I don't know what others know, I don't know what I'm doing

Believing we need to know what others know is us not knowing what we are doing. Others know what's useful to them. What's useful to you is knowing how to be less like others and more like yourself. Knowing what you know is more than enough to get you to knowing the next thing you need to know to get you to the next thing you need to know. That's what's

great about life, you have what you need, you know what you need to know, so it's great to be you, and you know enough to be great.

I have not achieved as much as others

You think achievement is a measure of ones worth in life. You are attached to needing this because you need to count in life, to matter and be regarded as important. Rather avoid the need to be counted and to be important. It's far more important to not need to be counted by others but by yourself. "You are more than important, but being counted by others is not."

Money makes the world go around

People have a "need" for more money because they believe it is a substitute for self-love and wellbeing. Yet the pursuit for more money is leaving you and the planet with less. The secret is to focus on Realizations of Truth. They bring more clarity, more wisdom and more money for all. The attainment of money doesn't have to mean great sacrifice on Earth. Chase realizations not money, and there will be no more sacrifice just more gain. Realizations are a currency that keeps on giving to you, the Earth and all that dwell within.

Life is always difficult

Some of us believe life takes away your joy. But life keeps on giving you just have to be open to receive. It's you who takes away your joy to protect yourself from the threat of life taking joy away. You don't fear what life will do. You fear what you will do. Realise, taking away your own joy doesn't make you safer, just sadder, and no one can take away joy if you don't. The best form of self protection is to keep and hold onto what brings you joy. Life wants you to allow in more joy not less.

The more I do the more I have in my life

When you focus on creating more in your outer reality you take from your inner reality; your health, sanity and overall wellbeing. If you focus on your

inner reality, what it needs and by seeing how much you already have, and then working on yourself to see how much more you already are, you can't help but create more in your outer reality. See more in your inner reality and you will experience more in your outer reality. You are already so much more than you can see in you right now.

Money is hard to come by

Money is not hard to come by or hard to make. What's hard is allowing yourself to make money in an easy self-nurturing way. You think it has to take great sacrifice and effort. It's only hard when you try to do it the way everyone else is trying to do it. You have a true path for wealth and success, it's about living your life purpose. Follow that and money will follow you wherever you go. If you don't believe you are entitled to it, it becomes difficult to make. Living your purpose has you be entitled to it. The Universe gives to you when you give back to it, that you can expect. Be your purpose, don't just live it, BE it!

It's acceptable for a business to harm the environment to make money

If it's acceptable for the business to harm the environment then what you are saying is it's acceptable for the business to cause harm to us all. We see environmental impacts as the cost of doing business and making money. But ignoring the environment to make money has an even greater cost to profits. When a business shifts from focussing on profits into how can it give to back to the Earth, profits skyrocket. Those who align to the needs of the Earth receive the most support from the Earth. The more you keep giving back, the more you earn.

I haven't done a good enough job in my life

Life is not a race, where you compare how you go with others. It's not about how well you perform, how well you achieve or how well you out smart everyone else. There are no others, there is only you! You feel you haven't done a good enough job because you are still comparing yourself

against others. Comparing is you not doing a good enough job at being self-loving. You can be proud that you stepped out of the race, that's more than a good enough job.

I don't like what I have in my life

We were taught as children, to dislike what we have in order to get something different. As a child if you dislike what you were given you'll receive something else. Disliking yourself, which is what's really going on, won't get you to like yourself even more. You believe by disliking yourself will somehow have you improve. Disliking yourself stops you from seeing how great you really are and creating more great things in your life. It's liking yourself that gives you exactly what you're looking for in life, which is to like yourself.

I can't like myself the way I am

We learnt as children that you should only like yourself if you are making no mistakes, behaving right and ultimately being perfect human being. We look at ourselves and see many issues. But what we didn't know was that having many issues is us being perfect. It means we are on the playing field giving life our best go. Accept issues as perfect, and like yourself for being perfect.

The more things I do that I dislike the bigger the reward at the end

We believe that if we slog ourselves and work hard doing what we'd rather not do, that the reward at the end will be more of what we do like. Many lives are misspent and even lost this way. The reward in doing is meant to be during the doing not at the end. To love what you are doing gives you the reward of experiencing love now not later. If you postpone love until the end, there is no love to sustain you through the now. What kind of life is that? When you give yourself love now, you'll be creating more experiences of love in the future.

I feel guilty putting myself first

Many of us were taught that other people are more important than we are. We learnt that pleasing them first has us feel that we are ok as we are. Realize doing more for others will have you feel good and sometimes really good but doing more for yourself will have you feel great about yourself. You don't need others permission to feel great about yourself.

I need money

Money is very useful, no doubt, but 'needing' money, stops money from coming to you. See you already have plenty of money and it will flow far more effortlessly. To need it comes from believing you don't have any. Believing you don't have any creates you not having any. The Mind needs money you have an abundance of it.

I have to do something right to feel good about myself

We were taught as children that you can feel good about yourself if you do something well or get something right. In other words we learned that feeling ok about ourselves has to be earned. The more good things you do the more you have earned the right to feel ok with yourself. You could feel good about yourself for realising you no longer need to earn the right to feel good about yourself. Now feel good about yourself for feeling good about yourself.

I need to be free and feel free in my life

Many of us crave greater freedom in our lives, but is this freedom from what we think? The freedoms you crave are actually less about other people, places or situations but more about needing to get away from how you think about yourself and your life. You seek freedom from being mean to yourself, from always putting pressure on yourself to be a somebody or get somewhere. When we stop assessing how far we have got in life, when we stop assessing if we are doing a good job, when we stop the threat of bad judgement for ourselves, we will be free.

You will like yourself a lot more without judging whether your likeable yet or not.

What I have isn't enough, I need more

Feeling this way comes from not ever stopping long enough to take stock of everything you are and everything you have. Because we neglect to notice ourselves, we expect others to. The way to create more in this Universe is by first noticing how much you already are and how much you already have.

Making money is stressful and I don't want more stress

What we don't want in our life is to strive for money but to fail in the process. This fear of failing stops us from trying in a way that would actually succeed. You don't want to feel like a failure so don't strive for more money rather strive to notice something about yourself you've never noticed before. That is, that you are lovable even without money. If you can love yourself without much money, then you can love yourself through creating it.

I don't deserve lots of money

What we don't deserve in life is to be without money. But we are taught money takes deserving, earning, trying, fighting, succeeding and so on. Actually, making money takes doing what nobody else can do better than you, and that's be you. That's the real blockage here, is the belief you don't deserve to be the real you, and live the life you want. Only you deserves this, no one else.

I don't have money

This is a nasty belief that prevents an inflow of money. You need to see that everyone of us has a bank account put a side by the Universe. It has our name all over it. So, you 'have' money you just haven't learned how to make a withdrawal. It comes down to seeing that all you are, is all you will ever need to experience a great life. We call this self-belief. You've got what it takes for your own life … nobody else could do a better job, and nobody is asking more from you than that.

I hate what money does to me

Money can lead to stress, arguments and even wars. Or is it rather the absence of money that leads to these things? Money is a measure of how much self-belief you have, of how much self-worth you have. A high self-worth creates a high net worth, a low self-worth creates a low net-worth. It's not what money does that you hate, it's actually what a low self-worth does to you, you 'hate'. Stop hating money and you'll have more of it. Stop hating yourself and you'll have more of EVERYTHING!

I hate the rich

Many of us are raised to dislike and mistrust wealthy people. This leads to us blocking the flow of money because we don't want to dislike and mistrust ourselves. What you dislike is that you were mislead about money, how to make it, and what it means to have it. You hate that you believed what others said rather than discovering your own truth about having money. You dislike that you see yourself separate from money when all this time you could have seen yourself as money itself.

I hate spending money

It's not spending money we dislike, it's making ourselves wrong for spending money, that we dislike. We have become scared of ourselves over the years. No one yells at us, punishes us, criticises us or blames us the way we do. We worry if we spend money unwisely we will come down on ourselves so hard we will end up hating ourselves. In truth what we really dislike is that we see money as more important than we are, enough to put ourselves down for it. It's valuing money more than us that hurts, so next time you are spending money have it be because you are valuing yourself, and you'll be ok.

I don't want to be seen as successful

One of our biggest blockages to creating success in life is we worry what we will become when successful. We've heard people becoming arrogant,

not caring about what matters anymore, ignoring friends and so on. But what is more terrifying than all that is the reason we want to become successful in the first place. It's our reasons that frighten us, not other people's reasons. Have success mean life becoming more simple and you will have nothing to fear.

People will criticize me if I am successful

Fear of criticism is very dauting. We worry that the larger the spotlight on us the more people looking at us and the more criticising us. But criticism isn't actually your biggest fear, it's loathing yourself. What if you finally get to being successful and it fixes nothing? What if you still are depressed, still dislike yourself and are still unhappy? A scary thought, right? Don't aim for success to fix your problems, aim to fix your problems because that's you achieving success.

I won't be wanted if I am successful

We've all been told it's lonely at the top. So many of us fear losing friends and having no-one to relate to the more successful we become. What this points to is how lonely you are now, that you are not even in your own corner backing yourself with love and appreciation. If you want yourself now you won't worry about not being wanted into the future. Wanting to want yourself makes you very easy to want.

I'll lose myself if I am successful

How many times have you heard someone say they are going to find myself, or I have lost myself in relationship. The truth is you are lost right now. You lost yourself years ago that's why it shows up as a fear because you worry you will do it all over again and suffer again as you did many years ago. You got lost as soon as you believed I need a self. Life is not about finding your-self but realising you never needed one in the first place.

I can't imagine myself as a success

Life has been tough for many of us. It can be hard to imagine ourselves with any real success. But we find it easy to imagine ourselves with more failure don't we. This is because the person, the I, you imagined yourself as, was the original "failing". By imagining a self, a person with an identity we failed to see we never had an identity and were better off without it. Rather than trying to imagine yourself as a success, imagine what you are without a self, because this is the ultimate success.

People will hate me if I am rich and successful

What do you hate about yourself now, is the question? Do you hate that you even want to be rich and successful? Yes. Does it upset you that you can't love yourself as you are right now? Yes. Needing to be more than you are right now hurts, and we don't like hurting ourselves. Realize that needing this and many other things wasn't what will bring happiness, but it is what's stopping you from being happy now.

I am more comfortable with failure than being a success

Failure and disappointment have become the norm for many of us. So much so than when they aren't happening, we can't help but create them to feel safe. We like predictable so we create it. We feel safe with failure because we can't fall any lower. But what we love even more than the predictable, is being surprised by our own greatness. Decide – "I am going to surprise myself today, by staying away from the familiar". Because even though the you, you think you are is familiar you'd be surprised to know it's not you at all. Intend to meet the unfamiliar you (the real you), and you'll live an unfamiliar life.

I like to make my life difficult to feel successful

Many of us confuse overcoming challenges with achieving success in our lives. But achieving success is more about overcoming the right challenges, not just any challenge. Overcoming the need to complicate our life is one

such challenge. Success is keeping life simple, not making life harder than it needs to be. When you create simplicity, you are creating success.

If I am busy I am succeeding

Like the above, many of us confuse busyness with success. But busyness for the sake of being busy rarely creates any favorable outcomes. We believe that busy equals productive, and sometimes it does. But stillness over busyness fast-tracks our growth and success because it is the stillness where inspiration is received. Inspiration is not of the Mind but beyond it, coming direct from the Universe to you. Be still before being busy, it makes being busy far more successful.

If I am not successful I won't be respected

Many of us crave respect from others so we set ourselves the goal of being successful. We want the experience of being respected so that we can feel ok within ourselves. We do not feel respected now, not because others don't respect us and not because we are not successful, but because we think we need to be successful to respect ourselves. We want self-respect, but we have put an obstacle on our path, the need to be successful. Realise, it is far more respectable if you remove obstacles to self-love rather than adding them.

I need to be successful so I don't regret my life

Being "successful" in our society has come to mean many things. The most common interpretation is to be wealthy and admired for having achieved what you set out to achieve. It makes sense to the Mind that this is a great way to avoid regretting one's life. Except for one small detail. Who said we would regret our life if didn't take the "successful path"? We worry we will regret our life, not because of what we will or will not do, but because of what we have already done. We regret never having gotten to know who we are, just rather accepting what the Mind says we are. We regret substituting the Mind for our-self. But it's not too late to learn who you really are, and you'll discover you're not a who either.

I need success to have me feel a whole person

The I needs, you do not. Whenever you become aware of a thought "I need" come to understand that this is the Minds need. The I and the Mind are one, but you are neither of these. By believing you are the Mind, the I, you experience what it experiences, needs insecurities, jealousies, the lot! The Mind wants to feel whole because it's a void, but you are already whole, just not a whole person, but a whole Universe. The Universe never needed an I to be a success, therefore neither do you.

I fail before I even begin

It's very easy for many of us to expect a failure outcome. We were criticized so much as children we learnt we can fail right from the start. We were taught our ideas were all bad. And despite our best efforts to believe in ourselves and our ideas, we still launch ourselves into a project believing - all my ideas are bad, and this will prove no different. But the failure was not our ideas but needing and relying on other people's thoughts and ideas about our ideas. "I need other people's ideas" was the failed idea.

I need people to like my ideas before I can like my ideas

As a child you always have an audience to impress. School mates, teachers, parents and relatives. Life starts a little unfair in that way as you learn to be a people pleaser to receive the love and attention you desperately crave. But here's what went wrong. What you didn't realize was they can't see you for all that you are, nor could they see your ideas for everything they were too. All they could see was whether you fit into their mold of reality. But you were never meant to. So, you come away feeling disappointed unless they agreed with everything you say think or do. The good news is the more disappointed they were in how you see the world the more you can come away with my ideas are next level. You were never meant to fit the mold and your ideas weren't meant to be understood by everyone. Your ideas are amazing and the only one the "need to amaze" is yourself.

I need my friends to support my ideas

It can hurt when you have a wonderful idea but others can't see it for its full potential. It has us feel rejected, an outcast, and often someone who is not as smart as everyone else. Your ideas are unique and it's only from you believing in them will they get to live out in the world. You have to believe in them today and not wait for anyone else to like them or trust in them. You have to trust in yourself now. You have to be a friend to yourself on this journey, be supportive, empowering, loving and encouraging just like a friend would. You be the friend to yourself, that you have been looking for in everybody else.

I'm not allowed to be successful

Do you ever feel like no matter how hard you try, how smart you are, that success is just not going to happen to you?

Many of us are brought up to despise people more successful or affluent than we are. As children we decide, I never want to be hated the way our parents hate successful people, so we vow never to attract our parents "hating attention" by standing out as a tremendous success. We promised ourselves we wouldn't do it, so we hold ourselves back in all areas without ever realizing it. In truth, 'people don't hate other people who are successful, they hate themselves for not being successful'. We worry we will do the same to ourselves. The remedy is to not need success to love yourself, but love yourself first, see just how important you are right now. That is the success beingness you've been searching for.

I have to be ashamed of who I am, of who I have become

Many of us have ideas about who we are meant to be when we are older, of how we are meant to act and behave. We imagine ourselves to be cool, calm and collected. We imagine no stress and no worries. We imagine contentment within our marriages and success in our life.

But when we do get a bit older and our view of our self now does not match who we thought we should be now, then there is trouble. We freak

out, we worry, we begin to break down and feel disappointed and even ashamed at ourselves. So, what's the truth? We are really ashamed that our view of ourselves was so much smaller than what we truly are. The reason we are ashamed is that we boxed ourselves into being like so many other people we have come across.

In fact, this boxing us in is the cause of huge meltdowns as we get older. We are nothing like who we imagined ourselves to be and holding to this vision is very constraining. It's better to be without a need to imagine yourself in anyway, no labels, no orientation, no constraints, just choices. You are free to be without an identity. You are free to be without an imagined self.

Everyone has to have an opinion on me and I better get that right

We believe that we invent how people see us, that we can engineer a good outlook. But what people see in us is less a reflection of what we have created and more to do with what they are willing to see in themselves. We exert very little influence in how others see us, and we have very little control over this. Yes, we crave change, but trying to change how others see us is a losing battle as it is beyond our control. Where we have the most control is over how we see ourselves, and that where our focus needs to go. It's needing others to change their view of us that has us feel bad about ourself. It makes life this constant battle. The real victory lies in realizing changing other people's opinion of you doesn't change your opinion of yourself. But changing your opinion of yourself is the change you've been looking for.

I need others to know I am right about things

It feels good to be right about things especially when you know things that others don't know. Uncommon knowledge is prized upon this Earth, so it is something many of strive for. But what is this really about?

We believe if what we know is right then what we believe about ourselves is right too. But this is "wrong". We need to be right about ourselves

because deep down we question what we believe. We are not here to be right about ourselves we are here to let go of being right about ourselves.

The amazing thing about all of us is there is no fixed knowledge about us, we are not finite being where we can learn all about ourselves. There are no concepts or descriptions that will give an accurate depiction of what we are. Rather be comfortable with the idea that we are not right about ourselves and that's a wonderful thing. In fact everything we have ever be**lie**ved about ourselves is false.

Let go of needing to be right about yourself and be open to discovering the immeasurable depth and expansiveness of your true being, never ending, always evolving, always becoming more. Allow in a bigger picture of yourself, because that's far more useful than being right about yourself. The irony is, how much we can see within ourselves determines how much we can see about all topics in the Universe.

I can't see myself as great, until I achieve greatness

It's easy to borrow from others what "greatness" looks like. We measure ourselves against the best of the best looking for that greatness in us and in where we stack up. But greatness isn't where you are like another. It cannot be seen through comparison.

Greatness is where you are unlike anyone else. That's where you really get to shine. And your greatness lies in being able to do this life, this mission, unlike anyone else in the world.

You can find your greatness by looking within yourself, at what you do differently to everyone else, in what makes you quirky, unique, baffling, Mind blowing, edgy, and in what makes you unrelatable.

We are all a unique idea from the Universe, each one an essential contribution that doesn't just exist on Earth but spans the depths and breath of the Universe itself. You are an idea that will make all the difference to your life, and all the differences on the Earth. You are the idea the Earth needs most right now. Be your idea, it's one of life's few guarantees of success.

The world doesn't want to see my kind of greatness

The Mind loves to externalize everything, making the problem exist outside of ourselves, rather than seeing the problem lies in the 'self'. We don't want to see our own greatness because it's different from the greatness we see in the rest of the world. We find it difficult to handle how different we are so we reject ourselves and our ideas before they can exist in the world. "I reject myself" is the belief hiding here. The problem came from the fact that we just never knew how different we were meant to be. If we knew, we'd be embracing ourselves right now, rather than rejecting ourselves for makes us different.

Know you are meant to be extremely different, radically different, on the verge of unrecognizable as a normal human being. You are meant to know and see things no one knows or has ever seen before or is even capable of knowing or seeing. Want to be this different and you will be extraordinary!

In truth what we want is to be unrecognizable to ourselves, not the same as everyone else. This is the greatness we really crave, so start letting it in.

I am hated

Many of us were shown as a child to hate ourselves. Our parents yelled and screamed at us and we learned how people see us. But the hatred we felt was not the hatred others felt about us but how they felt about themselves for mistreating us. Then we learned to hate ourselves every time we mistreat ourselves to. This occurred numerous times until we came to believe "I am hated".

What we hate is ever having hatred for ourselves and ever believing we were hated. Hatred is a sticky energy that locks into the body faster than nearly any other thought frequency on Earth. And it does more damage to our body and our life than any other thought frequency too. In fact when

we hate another person, that brings that persons energy into our body, causing all kinds of problems.

Realize, it's not me that is hated, it's hate itself. But we don't need to hate the hatred inside of ourselves because that just keeps it there. We can love that we were never this hatred. We are the love that's been hiding underneath the whole time. We are the love we have been searching for our whole life. What we hated was never believing we are love, refusing all this time to let it in. But we are not that hatred, we are not the void. The void hates itself for not being Love.

Thank goodness we ARE the Love.

If I have self-belief, it will be taken away from me

One of our greatest fears is what if I have self-belief and enjoy having self-belief, someone somewhere will cause me to doubt myself and I'll fall hard. We worry we will then question ourselves to the extreme until all the joy and self-confidence is drained out of us.

And that's your fear right there, not in what others will do to us, but how we will respond to what others have done to us. The fear is "What if I take it away, what if I keep taking my self-belief away?". Many of us have done it our whole life. We believe if we don't take it away first someone else will. But no one is here to take your self- belief away, but help you develop your own resilience to not taking away your own self-belief.

You are allowed to see yourself as more and amazing. You are allowed to enjoy your greatness. You are allowed to experiment without punishing yourself along the way. You are allowed to keep believing in your way of doing things. You are allowed to be what makes you unique. It's allowed. Confidence and self-belief comes from realizing you were never the need to have confidence or self-belief.

I have to be terrified of the outcomes I create

Many of us fear that we will create disasters in our own life, failure after failure, disappointment after disappointment. But what you are terrified of is not the outcomes you create but the outcomes others create in your life. You have nothing to fear from yourself. You create good outcomes when you trust and listen to yourself. Stay away from trying to please other people because that's when you don't create nice outcomes for yourself.

Ask yourself "what will please me right now?" And you can create amazing things. But needing to please others and sacrificing what pleases you will create disappointments for you time and time again.

The only way to be truly happy is to do for yourself what makes you truly happy.

Giving to yourself is what the Universe wants, that's why you are here so the Universe can give to itself. Self-Love opens those flood gates, not self-denial. The added benefit is that what makes you happy is also what will make many others happy as well. Trust that what you want is what the Universe also wants and make it happen.

I'm going to let myself down with everything I do

We think because we have made mistakes in our past that making mistakes is who we are. But the only mistake is identifying the outcomes we have experienced in life. We think we are what we create. If we create a successful outcome, then we are that success. If we create a failed outcome, we are that failure. But we are not these outcomes, that's not where we can be found. But if you are trying to find yourself by creating outcomes then you will experience yourself as the outcomes you create. You are looking for self-love by creating lovable outcomes. You are trying to measure yourself through an outcome. But the need to measure one-self is not self-loving, it's coming from self-doubt. No outcome can measure you, no matter how big or small. Instead of looking for yourself in each outcome of life, do things for the love at the start not for the love you may or may not give yourself at the end.

If you give yourself love at the start you guarantee yourself love at the end. Your level of beingness going in = your level of beingness coming out.

People will see through my greatness and find holes

We often worry our greatness is only skin deep and nothing truly substantial. We fear being pointed at, criticized, ridiculed and left feeling horrible about ourselves, as if we've been pretending to ourselves that we have real talent. So the belief here is actually "I'm without real talent". The truth is it takes talent to pay no attention to what others think of you. It takes talent to not compare yourself to others, it takes talent to see your uniqueness amongst a world of people yelling "look at me".

Many of us struggle to see what we have that is truly special, so we think we have no talent. But not seeing our talent doesn't mean we are without talent. We just don't believe we have the talent enough to see our own talent. So, we are the ones finding holes and missing our own greatness. It's just the Mind that says this is what everyone else is doing to us. Have the talent to persist with yourself to see what you've never seen before, that you never needed to have a talent to love yourself. Loving yourself is the most useful talent there is.

I have to scrutinize myself

Many of us make ourselves wrong for nearly everything we do, but why? Is it because we believe it will improve our life? Actually no. We often do it to make ourselves feel terrible as a form of protection. We expect someone else will make ourselves feel terrible about what we do so we get in first. We believe "if someone is going to be mean to me I need to get in first so it's not as painful". Furthermore, we also believe if we get in early then at-least we are agreeing with them in part, to avoid feeling like a complete outcast. We were taught it's better to agree with something even if it's painful if it means we will avoid a greater pain of being unliked and unwanted.

Be an outcast, be unafraid to stand out like a sore thumb, by no longer needing an opinion about yourself. Don't aspire to be liked, aspire to be

unlike who you've always thought you should be, starting by getting rid of all your opinions about yourself.

I'm going to look very bad at the end of this

Through our upbringing we have become very afraid of what we look like to others, on how we will be seen by the outside world. We question "what will others think of me?" Will I be made to feel alone, unpopular, not clever enough?" "Will I be left feeling like a reject who never does anything as well or as professional as anybody else?"

We are worried we will be shown up to be mediocre as many of us already fear we are. We believe "I'm nothing special" so we worry we will always be seen as nothing special.

What there is to realize is, winning people over is nothing special. It is a very mediocre achievement at best. It's especially mediocre winning over highly critical, judgmental and skeptical people, because those who judge and criticize are being nothing special.

You on the other hand, are the one taking bold risks, achieving the unachievable, and being a believer that you are worth more than the label – mediocre. You are already what you've been searching for ... you are already what you were hoping others would see in you first.

You are the special someone you had always hoped to be. You are life changing. Trying to look good for others has you look bad to yourself.

I need to make a difference

Needing to make a difference drives us to keep finding new ways to feel we are doing our bit in our family and on the Earth. And when we aren't doing our bit, we feel very discontent and struggle within ourselves. But, believing we are all here to be of service to others often leads us to be of no service to ourselves. Making a difference begins with ourselves. Being of service begins with ourselves.

The Mind says making a difference starts with others, so it urges us to focus our efforts and energy on others. But then we get neglected, so if we all neglect ourselves trying to make a difference there will be a lot of us neglected. We are the others in this world, we all make up the world so all of us need to be given to. If we all made a difference to ourselves, there would far less people left that still need a difference made to them.

The difference you are looking to make is to yourself, to love yourself just as you are without needing to make a difference to anyone else first. You deserve your love, first.

A Word From Your Sponsor....

Going Deeper...

The person I believe myself to be is who I really am

Ever since we were very young, we have been seeking answers to a very important question: 'Who am I?' This question emerged as our awareness began to grow within the womb. What we were aware of was nothing short of incredible. It was nothingness, a space without the Mind. This infinite awareness started making its way into our tiny vessel of a body. It was bliss.

Unfortunately, this bliss and expansive awareness was very short-lived as we began to feel and notice the things all around us. Our attention was drawn to thoughts and feelings, but they were not ours; they were those of our parents.

So small and sensitive, we could feel what they were thinking, their fears, their beliefs, and their concerns about bringing a new life into this world safely and successfully. We felt a prolific energy all around us, much more intense than what we could feel within us … it was the energy of an Identity.

We began questioning what we are and whether we need to be more like others around us. We felt how they saw themselves; small, finite, having this identity full of labels and beliefs.

It didn't take long before the very first thought entered our brain – "I".

This "I" thought had a unique character to it. It was a substance that meant – "whatever you believe about yourself you are". But to believe we are this I meant shifting from what we knew to be our infinite nature into something empty, in other words a void that wanted to be filled with beliefs. A void, that for the next twenty years or so, would draw more thoughts of doubt and uncertainty about ourselves to it, like a black hole.

Having this "I" began our quest to learn and discover who we are. As we grew up, we listened and watched what others said about us, how they felt about us. We reacted to who we were and what we did, and we began believing things about ourselves. These beliefs that we have accumulated since the womb now form the very basis of our entire identity, but they are not about us; they are about the void within us.

Realize: "I am not the uncertainty inside of me; I am the awareness of the uncertainty and always have been!"

The Mind is who I am; the Mind is who we all are

We have been experiencing the Mind for so long that we have come to assume that what we feel, think, and believe about ourselves is the Truth. Let us face it, who told us otherwise? Mom and Dad, despite their best efforts, were often telling us who we are, what we are good at, not good at, whether we were loved or a total disappointment.

We learned very quickly to listen and trust in what they had to say about us. And the more they said, the more the beliefs kept accumulating, one after the other: 'I am a nuisance'; 'I make life harder'; 'I need to impress others to get love'; 'I only get attention if I am sick'; 'I do not count as an equal around here'; 'I am a mistake'; and so on.

Then there were teachers at school whose job was to empower us with new knowledge and skills. But during test time and exams, we quickly learned who we are in this world by our grades. We either believed we were smart and going to be successful, or average, or worse, destined to be failures and unimportant our whole lives. We learned how hard we had to work to keep up and make the cut. We learned whether we were fast learners or slow learners, whether we were like everybody else or nothing like anybody else.

And let us not forget our social circles. We gained a very clear insight into whether we were interesting, desirable, attractive, relevant, important, noticed, a true somebody, or worse—a complete nobody. All these

experiences, and all the beliefs that came with it, are all recorded in the Mind. So, who do you think you are? I am here to tell you; it is not who you actually are.

"The Mind and the Identity are one, but I am neither of these. I am what came before the Mind."

Everybody believes they are the Mind, so I will too

We learn a lot about how life works and how we are meant to live from those around us and from those we see in the media, movies, and TV. Unfortunately, many of the examples we grew up with have taken us off-course, away from what is true and correct and into what everyone believes is true and correct. What makes this really challenging is the belief that the more people believe something, the more it must be true.

As we grew up, we witnessed virtually everyone around us believing they were the contents of their Mind. We saw people constantly using labels to define themselves—rich, poor, good, bad, successful, failures, healthy, unhealthy, attractive, ugly, smart, dumb, and the list went on. We heard people use labels to define us, and guess what? We caught on quickly and started doing the same.

We learned that to label and define ourselves was how life worked on planet Earth. Everybody was doing it, so we thought it was right. But this way of life did not improve our lives. It just made them harder, more upsetting, and more of a struggle, because labels take far more away than they give. Once you label and define yourself, you get to experience that label and the limits of that definition in all areas of life.

We end up believing that if everyone is calling themselves their Mind, we should too. What we did not see at the time was that everyone was struggling because of it—not necessarily on the outside, but definitely on the inside. Labels hurt because they are part of the void. The irony is that everybody is trying not to label themselves but actually trying to rid themselves of their labels. They go about it in the incorrect way, but still, all

everyone wants is to not feel the way their labels make them feel. They just want to feel good about themselves.

"Doing what everyone else does has me feeling the same as everyone else feels—not happy!"

The way to feel better about yourself is to want more and have more

By the time we were teenagers, we had accumulated hundreds of beliefs about ourselves—some of us thousands. And so, the void within that began all those years ago was not actually getting fuller, just emptier with every new belief we added. We thought the more we knew or believed about ourselves, the more whole we became...but instead we felt worse about ourselves.

What is the remedy to feeling not enough, inadequate, unimportant, unnoticeable, unlovable, and worse? Well, in the past we have taken our cues from what others were doing to make themselves feel better—and what a buffet of options we saw: alcohol, drugs, sex, ambition, achieving, spending, being competitive, standing out from the crowd, and more. You name it, the world has figured out how to conquer the blues. But all these options have something in common. They require something outside of ourselves to fix something that is going on inside of ourselves.

The world believes the solution to all our woes is to be found outside ourselves: in others, substances, recognition, money, hurting ourselves—in everything but not within ourselves. That was overlooked. We learned that the more we have, the happier we will be—so we strive for more. We learned that the more liked we are by others, the more we can like ourselves. We learned that the fitter and healthier we become, the less we have to look at how we feel on the inside. We learned that the more we numb our pain with drugs and alcohol, the better we feel. But all these things do not change what we believe about ourselves; they just offer temporary relief.

The way to heal the void is not to do what the void is telling you to do, or what the void has been telling everyone else to do. Rather, the way

forward is to heal the contents of the void—to heal the beliefs with a magical substance called Truth.

The void has always been non-truth, and so the Mind began as non-truth. So whatever it says to do to fix yourself, is also going to be non-truth. This is where Enlightenment comes into play. It is the healing of the void through the realization of Truth.

"When I stop doing what everyone else does, I will stop deepening the void and will set myself free."

Enlightenment takes too long and is too difficult

The journey of Enlightenment is greatly misunderstood. It is perceived as nearly impossible and therefore, a waste of time. This journey is meant to seem impossible. It is meant to seem like the hardest possible milestone a human being can achieve. Enlightenment has that reputation. It is deliberately this way, so you give up on it and go back to the life you have always known. The void says it is too hard, but that is because it is made of different matter. It is too difficult for the void, but for you it is what you already are.

Ironically, what is harder than achieving Enlightenment is living without it. Life full of all your beliefs is much more difficult. The trick is to see that settling for the contents of the Mind as the Truth makes life virtually unbearable. Even though these beliefs seem like they represent you, they do not even belong to you. They do not reflect you in any way; in fact, they reflect who you are not. They are everything you are not. The more you see them as not you and not belonging to you, the faster they will disappear.

"Before the void, I saw myself as infinite, and I can easily get back to that ME."

Enlightenment will take away what is important to me

It may be confronting to hear it, but you are already taking from yourself by seeking the unimportant in life. Enlightenment is realizing what is actually important and prioritizing your life around what gives, nurtures, and brings joy.

How much of your life is spent caring how you appear in the world, what others think of you, whether they approve of you, or whether you are seen as important and relevant? How much of your life is spent in hectic energy, racing around doing as much as you can rather than being still in the moment and enjoying being you?

Another term for Enlightenment is self-love. So, a life lived from a space of self-love is an Enlightened life. You will notice that children are very good at this. They are always in the moment; they desire joy, affection, hugs, and lots of play; and they do not put off love for some time in the future. They understand intimacy at the deepest level, and they are unafraid to ask for the love they need.

As adults, we push, strive, and work more than play. We worry, we put ourselves and our needs last, we concern ourselves with what others think of us, we believe we are not good enough, and we do not believe we are worthy of receiving self-love. The Truth is, we are taking from ourselves in more ways than we know. Believing we are someone we are not takes away from us the most.

Enlightenment is receiving on every level. It is the ultimate in giving back to yourself.

Realize: "I cannot afford to delay what I need most in my life."

Enlightenment will mean the end of who I am striving to be

We are told that the more we try and the harder we work, the better a person we will become. And so we work hard our whole lives, putting more and more pressure on ourselves to improve. We study, read book after book, take course after course, hoping we will become a better person because of it. We are told that one day we will be proud of who we are, and others will be proud of us too. Notice how the Mind puts the payoff in the distant future.

The Truth is you are already more now than you could ever hope to become. You always have been. It is your need to be more, your belief that

you are insufficient the way you are, that blinds you from seeing who you are on the inside.

Everything you aspire to be, you already are. You just believe that you are your beliefs instead of believing you are the Truth. Truth is all around us, showing us who we really are. Nature is truth; it is our nature. And so, our nature is infinite; it is everywhere and everything; it is beautiful, awe-inspiring, compassionate, loving, divine, creative, supportive, nurturing and wise. We are all that we see around us. Enlightenment is finally figuring this out.

So stop searching for yourself in what you do, in what you achieve, or fail to achieve. Stop searching for yourself in how others see you. You are not to be found there. Become aware of yourself wherever there is Truth. This is you. When you take away who you are striving to be, you will be Enlightened.

Enlightenment will not work for me—I want more in life

We all want more in life, but the old success formula of the more I DO, the more I will HAVE and the happier I will BE, takes more from us than it can ever give. The strategy of having more to make yourself happier is the very reason you are unfulfilled and still seeking more in life. It is a vicious cycle: Doing more only leads to exhaustion, stress and illness. Having more does not change what we intrinsically believe about ourselves, leaving zero increase in our state of BEing.

Turn the formula upside down, and it works much better. The true path is Be, Do, Have. When you are BEing self-loving, you will need to DO less to HAVE infinitely more! If you change your state of BEing at the start, you cannot help but create more in all areas of life. And how you will BE at the start of anything is how you will BE at the end. You cannot expect a new beingness from doing and having. To have more, you must see yourself as more from the start.

When you see yourself as a success, you cannot help but have successful ideas, create successful actions, and therefore create successful outcomes. Enlightenment is seeing yourself with fresh eyes. That is the work we are doing right here, right now, with the power of Truth—we are changing the way you see yourself. This expands your state of BEing, which expands the quality of your DOing, which in turn expands the quality of what you HAVE.

In Truth, it is not that you wanted more in life; it is that you have always wanted to see yourself as more.

Realize: "Wanting more in life is not working for me. Seeing how much I already am, is the secret to expanding my life."

I know who I am! I know myself very well

We may not think we are experts in many things in life, but one thing many of us believe is that we are experts when it comes to ourselves. We are convinced we know who we are.

Surprisingly, this is the least area we have expertise in. The you that you believe you are does not even come close to who you really are. We feel we know ourselves based on our personality, our reactions and quirks, our achievements, net worth, jobs and careers, how many friends we have, and who we know. We look for ourselves in our religion, decisions, mistakes, failures and victories. Even though we believe we know ourselves, we are still looking for ourselves everywhere, but where we can truly find ourselves.

The Truth is, we have never known ourselves, which is why we have not stopped looking for ourselves. We have made up a version of ourselves because we saw everyone else doing the same. This robbed us of the deepest self-appreciation and love, leaving an ever-gaping hole inside of us. To mend this, we have been looking for OUR love in all the wrong places—in money, people, and in our Mind-made identity, the void.

We have never been experts when it comes to ourselves; we are merely experts in trying to find ourselves.

"I will never truly know myself while I try to find myself. When I stop searching, I will realize there was never a self to find—just the love inside, for that is the real me."

I must switch myself off from the spiritual and nonphysical

Science, science and more science is what the Mind, and those stuck in the Mind, use to avoid perceiving a nonphysical Universe. The Mind recognizes that if we see it is made of nature, it will cease to exist. The more spiritual and Enlightened we become, the less grip the Mind has over us and over the world as a whole.

Understand that the Mind is not individual; it is a collective consciousness, consisting of all Minds, at a specific—lower—frequency we all dial into. The Mind is collective but is experienced individually. It is an energy that has been on this Earth for eons, busy suffocating the light out of the planet. It wants to control the Earth's resources and to do that, it needs to control the Earth's inhabitants. The Mind is a measure of control over humanity, designed to starve people from seeing their spiritual origins, and as such their true greatness. To worship science over spirituality is one of the Mind's strategies to remain in control.

The Truth is that true science and spirituality are one. Science describes people's observation of the Universe's intelligence at work. Spirituality describes the very same intelligence, but rather than observing it, spirituality is about seeing yourself as this intelligence. The Universe demonstrates its limitless intelligence everywhere. It is the creator of all, and the masterMind behind all sciences, both those discovered and those yet to be discovered.

"Science is a label the Mind uses to describe something it had absolutely nothing to do with. Spirituality describes my true nature. I am at the heart of conscious knowing. Creation is Me."

What people think of me matters

Does it hurt, when you hear or read something nasty someone said or wrote about you? If so, this belief is responsible. First of all, why do we care what people think of us?

We care simply because we believe that if someone thinks it, it must be true on some level. What we do not realize is that it is only true for them, not true in a Universal sense. It is just what feels true to them. And because we instinctively doubt our own self-concepts (rightfully so) we put a lot of stock in what everyone else thinks of us. We are plugged into their reality believing they know better than we do.

The way out of this pattern is to stop believing that what you believe is true. Start with ceasing to believe that what you think about yourself is true. Once you no longer believe what you think is real, you will stop believing what everyone else believes too. How can you do this?

You must first want to. So let this belief—or *Mind Lie*—be about being okay to let that one go. We want to believe that everything we think is real, because we believe that is the way to protect ourselves from what everyone else thinks of us.

Ludicrous, right? It is exactly the opposite. No one ever told us that if we stopped believing in our opinions, we would stop caring what others think of us—because if they did, we would have stopped a long time ago. The Truth is, you have no real need to believe what you think is real. You have no need to hold onto your opinions any longer. Nor do you have any real need to keep believing your beliefs. Your opinions and your beliefs do not make you who you are; they stop you from being who you really are. Love is what is real, if people do not have love for you than what they have for you is not real. The same goes for you. If you have opinions about you other than love, these are also not real.

"I never needed to believe in what I think, because what I think about myself, others, and the world is not what I really think—it is just what others already think. What I really think is not called thinking; it is

called loving. Loving is what I really do, not thinking. When I experience thoughts other than love, I am revisiting the opinions of others."

Realize: "I do not need to think of myself to find myself. Love is a higher vibration than thinking."

Focusing on money is more important than focusing on Enlightenment

This commonly held belief causes people all over the world to miss the biggest money secret on Earth. It is responsible for all those in the world who have spent their health trying to create wealth and now need to spend their wealth trying to regain their health.

Many make the mistake of leaving Enlightenment until a later stage in life, when all the assets have been accumulated and all the wealth created. But remember, to follow the void does not fill the void; it only deepens it.

Why gamble with Enlightenment when you can have security and certainty from focusing on money—after all, that is what everyone else does, right? The oversight is that Enlightenment is realizing one's true greatness. It is a quantum leap in one's state of being. A high self-worth creates a high net worth. A low self-worth creates a low net worth.

So spending your life in a low self-worth trying to make money, is far less certain and far less secure than focusing on creating a high self-worth. Seeing money as more important than Enlightenment is seeing money as more important than you. Living life this way is the real gamble.

If you focus on making money, your life will be full of effort. If you focus on Enlightenment, you will make money effortlessly.

"I am more important than money."

I am my Mind

You are not who you think you are. Enlightenment begins when you awaken to the idea that you are far larger and far more than you have ever imagined yourself to be.

Maintaining that the Mind is the real you hides the Truth about yourself from you. If you believe that all you are is everything you believe you are, then you become limited to that—limited and defined by every belief you hold. That is what it means to see yourself as the Mind.

Your Mind can therefore be described as a recording of every decision you have ever made about what you think is true and real. But you are not this recording; you only believe you are. You are not every belief you carry with you. You are not your thoughts, your experiences, your knowledge and your past.

What is the Mind-made me versus the real me?

The giveaway is that a you that thinks about itself in such limited terms is not the real you and never was the real you. The real you does not think of itself, nor try to label or define itself; rather, the real you knows itself in terms of everything it is, as opposed to everything it is not.

Therefore, when you experience thoughts such as: 'I am not this', 'I am not enough of that', 'I need to be more of this', or 'I need to have more of that', it is not the real you thinking these things. It is the Mind thinking these things, and you are only eavesdropping.

Be aware of the Mind's thinking, as this will help to delineate the real from the made-up. The Mind wants to believe it is real, and it can be very convincing at times. But remember, you were never the Mind. You are the observer of all its thoughts, feelings, doubts, and insecurities. Just be the observer of such Mind activity, so you do not have to keep playing it all out as your life. Be aware of all sentences beginning with I, because they are actually not about *you.*

"Become aware of the stillness that is the real you; the Mind is all the other noise."

I am a human being

Since we were very young, we have been taught that what we are is human beings. It is how we have labeled ourselves as a species; it is how we have defined ourselves.

Being human is a label, and as we now know, labels are limited. The more you relate to this label—or any label— the more you limit or constrain yourself to the definition of that label. To be 'only human' is a limited idea that often has us believe that we have faults, are unworthy of love, need to keep up with others, were born of sin, are imperfect, and need to conform to belong and be accepted. This is what needing to be human feels like.

In Truth, being a human is but one idea of what you can choose to be. It is not the ultimate idea of what you are.

Set yourself free; open yourself to a deeper truth that you are not just a human having ideas, but an infinite idea of the Universe seeing itself as being human. Like you, the Universe has ideas. One of them was you, and everything you represent is inside that idea. You carry with you information and unheard knowledge—this is you as an infinite idea being.

Be open to experiencing an idea bigger than yourself, bigger than being human. It will not hurt you; it is the smaller ideas that hurt you. Discovering what idea you are is the ultimate success, fulfillment, and health strategy!

"I am the idea I have not had about myself yet."

I am small and insignificant

It is hard to see yourself as all that you are when you have been taught to see yourself as small and insignificant. To have a small idea or view about yourself is what makes you experience yourself as small or limited. We were taught to feel this way growing up—not by those who were truly great, but by those who felt insignificant themselves.

Your Truth is that you are a limitless being—or an idea being. Quite the opposite of small and insignificant!

Your level of significance is immeasurable, indefinable. This is a quality the Mind struggles with. It wants labels and definitions, and this is where the big struggle in life comes from. It is not that you are not significant, but that you keep trying to quantify your significance through proving and comparing. The problem lies in needing to measure and define in the first place. When you take a limitless concept and try to squeeze parameters, labels, and definitions around it, things will hurt. Always trying to define and label ourselves is what makes our lives hurt.

That is the Mind, for it realizes it is insignificant. Discard the need to feel significant; it will show you just how significant you truly are.

"The idea that I need to be more, is small and insignificant."

I need love

Many of us were denied the essential loving connection children are meant to receive in nature. This creates a big hole within us—and a very painful one at that. We then spend most of our adult lives trying to fill this hole to ease our immense pain. We do this through ambition—the drive to win, succeed, or destroy ourselves. It prevents some of us from ever being truly content in our relationships and keeps us forever seeking love and validation from other partners. But make no mistake, the pain is on the inside, and it will not be healed from needing more from others, getting attention, or filling our bank account with money.

The Truth is, a child does not actually need love from his or her environment in the way we have always believed. Instead, it just needs to be reMinded that it is love, rather than the thoughts and self-concepts surrounding it. When we were young, we decided that we must see ourselves like everyone else sees themselves. The healing comes from taking a giant view of ourselves—as the stars above, as the whole Universe itself.

It is not the enormity of what we are and what the Universe is that we find too hard to let in; it is the smallness we find overwhelming and insurmountable.

"I am the enormity of my Truth, nothing less."

I am nothing without my Mind

Letting go of the Mind, aka Enlightenment, is a profound accomplishment in human life. But one of the biggest obstacles to this is the 'Who am I without my Mind? I cannot exist without it.'

We have convinced ourselves that this is the Truth, but to be without the Mind is to be without suffering. In Truth, the bigger fear is being without all our wants, all the things we have convinced ourselves are important to us: achievement, avoiding failure, greater knowledge, respect, success, status, less regrets, and so on. It is the fear of letting go of these that stops so many on the path of Enlightenment.

We think our wants will make our life here on Earth totally worthwhile, so we hold onto them. But the underlying reason we have huge investments in these wants, is that we believe they will make us worthwhile as human beings. Everything you think you need to be happy, content and accomplished is actually keeping you from ever feeling happy, content, and accomplished.

You believe you are nothing without these needs. The Mind is needs, so to be without needs is seen as being without the Mind.

"I am not any of these needs."

"Needs do not make me stronger; they make me weaker."

"Needs do not make me happier; they make me feel like I have less in life."

"I was already more, before the Mind said I was otherwise."

Everyone else has a Mind

We have huge addictions to being like other people, to fulfilling our goals and ambitions, and to always strive for more in life. We even have addictions to suffering—to being without in life and being recognized for enduring, persisting and struggling. What we are most addicted to is the need to view life through a lens called the Mind. To belong, to fit in with everyone else viewing their life through the Mind, we must do the same.

The Truth is, there is no living through the lens of the Mind; there is only struggle. The Mind is the addiction to being without, to struggle.

As so many are living without on this Earth, we see it as the norm, as the starting point. But we could just as easily realize that being without, is the Mind itself. Being the Mind and experiencing life through the Mind gives us the experience of being without. It agitates us in the core of our being and motivates us to acquire, earn, achieve, and make up for the emptiness, through whatever means we have available.

The more you believe you are without, the more you experience that. The more you realize you are, the more you attract that experience into your life. See yourself as needing less, and you instantly become more.

"I never needed more in life, just to have less needs."

Life is always difficult

Many of us experience life as constantly difficult with occasional highlights of joy. It is, however, meant to be the other way around. What makes life so difficult is trying to be human. It is living with human belief systems that makes life a living hell.

For life not to be difficult, we need to be free from these beliefs and live as our Truth. The true you offers a much more fun life than the life you get from trying to fit in as a human being.

So why do we insist on having a difficult life? Because it cannot get any worse if it is already difficult. Many of us are so accustomed to hardship,

that when there is no hardship we worry, so we create it. Many of us withhold joy from our lives, because we feel that any moment someone or something in life will take away our joy.

We believe we cannot live life for a second without disappointment happening to us. We believe that life takes away our joy. But life keeps on giving; it always has and always will. We just have to be open to receive.

The Truth is, we are the ones who take away our joy, to protect ourselves from the threat of life taking our joy away. You do not fear what life will do, you fear what you will do.

Realize that taking away your own joy does not make you safer, just sadder. The best form of self-protection is to keep and hold onto what brings you joy.

"Life will not take away my joy. Life wants me to allow in more joy, not less. Life wants me to receive, not be without. If I do not take my joy away, no one else can."

I need money

How much of our life have we spent being distracted by the pursuit of money? Too much! And many would argue that the need for money is not a belief, but Truth. 'Well, of course I need money; that is how our world works,' we say to ourselves, 'Money buys us what we need to survive and thrive on this Earth, so of course we need money.'

Do not let it fool you— this belief actually has nothing to do with money itself; rather, it is all about the need for money. It is not about having money; but keeping you in a space of needing it, having you running around in circles chasing it.

The more you see yourself without something, the more prevalent the Mind becomes in your life. The Mind is inherently without. It represents everything you are not. And because you use money to survive, the Mind weaves its way under the guise of Truth, convincing you that

needing money is good. The more you believe you need money, the more you believe you will be motivated to get up and make some.

But needing money keeps you from having it. It is the identity—or the I—that needs the money; it is not you who needs the money. The I is how the Mind identifies itself: **I for identity.** The Mind is full of needs, but you are not. It is the Mind's need, not your need. To have more money requires having more Truth, not needing more money.

When you stop seeing yourself as the Mind, you will stop experiencing its needs. Rather, see yourself as all that is.

"Money IS Me."

I can fail at life

The fear of failure is one of the most debilitating fears there is. But is failure even real, or is it simply an invention of the Mind to stop you from realizing your greatness? The Mind uses labels to stop us in our tracks. It fears that one day we will see that we are beyond the Mind.

To label anything as failure is the failure. You are always learning and growing from life. You cannot fail, but the experience of failure comes from believing that failure is real, believing that you can fail at life. You can make poor choices, injure yourself, run out of money and ruin lives, but what makes these failures is the label you give to them. It is the judgment that it labels as a failure.

To say: 'I have failed' is the real failure.

When you become wiser from your experiences, there is no failure. To be awake and aware is a success. To dismiss and deny the lesson and growth would be the failure, if failure was possible.

We are obsessed with labels, judgments and making conclusions. Yet everything we learn takes us closer to what we set out to achieve in the first place. The tumbles when we are learning to walk bring us closer to walking.

The business failures bring us closer to what we really should be doing. The self-doubt brings us closer to learning the importance of self-belief.

Life is not about success or failure. It is about loving yourself no matter the outcome, knowing you will be there for yourself—win, lose, succeed, or fail. That is true success.

"I can live a far more successful life without all the judgment I give myself. Being there for myself is all the success I ever wanted."

I need to impress others

We are taught that the more others like us, the more they admire and approve of us, the better we feel about ourselves. And so, we were taught to seek approval from others.

But that which feels so good is not coming from others liking us; it comes from us liking ourselves. When we feel liked and approved of, we feel worthwhile and accomplished. We then see ourselves as likable by ourselves, and this feels amazing. There is no greater feeling in life, no more sought-after goal, than to like—and ultimately love—ourselves.

We seek self-love by looking outside ourselves to others. This keeps us from finding what we need most. Pleasing others is not sustainable and love from others is a poor substitute for self-love. Needing others this way does not lead to self-love—it leads to self-pity, because to need others to like you is not what you consider to be likable about you. So, it is self-rejection.

Do something likable for yourself, and you will experience being liked, because self-love comes from being self-loving. You are lovable because you have love within you. This love you have for people, places, animals and experiences is also the love you have for yourself.

So, do you really need to impress others, or are you trying to impress yourself so you can see just how worth loving you really are? Remember, there are no others, just Minds—behind these Minds there is only love. We

are all love on the inside. What is more lovable than discovering that all this time you were made of love?

"I am the love hidden away beyond the Mind. I am all the love there is, and that is what makes me easy to love."

My body is frail and will become unwell

We have been taught that illness and disease can strike at any moment. We have been taught that our bodies are weak, and we are powerless to cure many illnesses. But it is not the body that is frail; it is frail thoughts and beliefs that make the body frail.

The body is made of Truth, but the Mind is non-truth, and so it hurts and ages the body. The body reflects the Mind and shows up our beliefs as a physical or emotional symptom. Therefore, our beliefs are at the root cause of virtually every illness we experience.

The cures to the world's deadliest illnesses exist not in the body, but in the Mind. To heal the body, you must heal the Mind. The longer you live from the Mind, the weaker your body becomes. Return to Truth and your body will thank you for it.

Beliefs are non-truth, and denying our greatness is also non-truth. But inside the body is information, knowledge, skill, and abilities that you are here to share. Inside of you is Truth, your message for the planet. To share this message is to share your greatness; this is to live your Truth.

Living your message, feeling it, hearing it, and delivering it, is the secret to healing and remaining youthful. Interfering with or doubting the value and worth of your message is a frail way to live. Seeing yourself as your message is the ultimate way to live.

"I am an infinite message of clarity and wisdom, worthy of being expressed."

I am worried I will see myself as a fraud

One of the biggest reasons we do not take risks and pursue our dreams in life, is that we are worried we will see what we have been worried about our whole life—that we are a disappointment, failure, fraud, unlovable, unwanted, unworthy, and untalented, a nobody.

What if you get shown up—what if others finally see who you really are? What if you see who you really are—and worse, what if you believe it? What if you see all these horrible things about yourself?

These are debilitating fears.

But what if you see marvelous things about yourself? How will you feel then? What if you see just how amazing you are and how much you have been living small by holding yourself back all your life? What if you see you were never any of these things in the first place, and you've wasted your life believing they were all you and true? Seeing your greatness can be just as scary as seeing your failures.

Realize your biggest fear is that you will spend your life holding yourself back. Let it go now, knowing that there is no risk in moving yourself forward only in holding yourself back. You have nothing to lose when being great just from being small. Your greatness has a time and a place, and that is now!

"I have not wasted myself; I have just been thinking I was someone else this whole time. The fraud is believing I am my thoughts, that I am the Mind—the Truth is knowing I was never the person I feared I was."

Money is the root of all evil

Money is very useful on this planet however, it is often a tool the Mind uses to distract us from seeing who we really are. It convinces us we cannot live without it, and then it tells us it is the root of all evil. Interestingly, believing this about money leaves you with none. Self-hate is the root of all evil, not money.

Many of us are without a lot of money because of how we see money. Some of us believe it is evil and creates wars, conflicts, and divorce, while others believe money does not like them, they are unlucky with money, they cannot be trusted with money, and so on.

Money is just energy that we believe gives value to our life on Earth. It is evil to believe you have a monetary value and are worth only the money you make or have. It is cruel to see yourself in this way. You are more valuable than money.

To believe that money makes you someone is not your Truth. It is what you do with money that gives money value. Money values you when you value yourself. Realize that money does not create your value. To set your value with money is to devalue yourself. Love makes your value. Love is eternal, love is infinite, love is beyond a value.

As the infinite there is no value that can be placed on you.

"I don't need to place a value on myself, because there was never value in having a Self."

I need more things, so I need to keep buying more things

Shopping has become a way to fill the void when you feel most empty. It provides temporary relief for the lack of fulfilment we are experiencing in life, for everything we have missed seeing about ourself.

Rather than trying to add to yourself with more things that end up being suffocating in your life, see that this emptiness is coming from the need to compare what you have with what others have.

We compare because we once believed that we should be more like others, and to be more like others we must have what others have. And so, we secretly promised ourselves that one day we will be like everyone else and have what everyone else has, and even more. But that is an empty promise, because you cannot be just like others—so it leaves you feeling empty.

The Truth is, you cannot be like others, nor will you ever see yourself like others. You feel sad that you made that promise to yourself and have been trying to honor it. You are upset at yourself for ever thinking you were not enough.

Forgive yourself for this promise. It is what you thought you needed, to see yourself as enough in life. See how much you are nothing like others, and you will feel so much fuller within yourself. The more you take away the need to be like others, the less things you need in your life.

"I promise not to be anything like others ever again. I am everything they are not, and I am everything I was meant to be. I never needed an 'I' the same as everyone else has."

I need to need

We have all come to believe that there are things we need. This keeps us striving, working hard, comparing ourselves, and being overly critical with ourselves. We do not stop to heal this, because it is what everyone else is doing too, which makes needing it seem even more normal and acceptable.

We see what others get from having more needs—they get more money than we have, more respect and admiration, vacation homes, comfort, luxury, better cars, and they get to feel richer, more successful, and more desirable than we do. And that is what we are after—the feeling that needs promise us. It is not so much the things we need, but what they stand to offer us.

We are desperate to heal from feeling unloved, unsuccessful, unworthy, undesirable, unimportant, unlucky, insignificant and unproductive. We deeply desire some of the good feelings we see others having about themselves.

We believe that desiring things will bring us feelings of success and accomplishment, value and importance. Yet keeping these feelings away, is the belief that we were never these things in the first place, and that to be

these things we must have needs. It is a vicious cycle from one need to the next, leaving us feeling more and more unfulfilled.

Yet we did not need to feel these things in the first place; we did not need needs in the first place. But there is a common belief that to exist is to need. The Truth is that we can move forward without having more needs. In fact, the less needs we have, the easier it is to move forward.

Existence requires being, not needing. There are no needs required in simply being. We are a 'being', not a 'needing'.

The next realization is that we never needed to strive to feel the way others feel about themselves. That was not a goal worth achieving, because it just created more needs. Realize that you never needed to put yourself down in the first place. You never needed to see yourself as less to create more in your life. That was not the strategy to become successful, it just filled you with more needs.

"The best gift I can ever give myself is to realize that these needs are not my needs; they are the void's needs. I can stop chasing after these needs. To need less and chase less, is true success."

"My need for having an I is lessening."

If I fear losing something that keeps it safe

In this world, we believe that to fear an accident, injury, or illness happening to someone we love, or even ourselves, is somehow the equivalent of protecting our loved ones or ourselves. If we are aware of a danger, and if we fear danger, we translate that to mean we are prepared for it or somehow better able to avoid it.

The Truth is, our fear does not protect anyone or anything, least of all ourselves. To love something is to protect it—but love in its true sense, not in the fear-based attachment experience of the word love.

If we love from a space of gratitude, that removes the fear of loss.

One of our biggest fears behind the scenes is that if we lose a loved one, it means we did not do enough. We did not protect them enough. Our fear then becomes about what we will say to ourselves, how we will blame and punish ourselves, and never be able to forgive ourselves.

But is that what we really fear? Or perhaps we fear that our neglect for ourselves is going to create some kind of loss in our own life. For instance, we might uncover beliefs about being irresponsible with ourselves; not caring for ourselves enough; or not being worthy of taking care of ourselves first.

What we really fear is losing ourselves. We fear realizing that we do not see ourselves as worth keeping in this life. We tell ourselves we are not worth saving. We are not special. We feel this way because we already lost ourselves, back when we decided that we are our thoughts, our Mind. So, we already have what we fear most.

So, what is the Truth?

"The best protection available is to let go of my identity rather than holding onto it. Holding onto my I is what I fear most."

If other people see me as great, that is better than seeing myself as great

We think others can see us better than we see ourselves, so if others think we are perfect then we can allow ourselves to see our perfection as well. But the perfection we seek is not actually perfection it is acceptance we crave, acceptance from others. This has you spend years grooming, improving, shaping, coloring, impressing, giving, compromising and comparing—all to one day have others recognize your perfection. You think this will allow you to see your own perfection, but this need prevents it instead.

You think seeing yourself as perfect eliminates all the flaws you see in yourself, a type of remedy to end your pain. But its needing to see yourself as perfect that has you see all these flaws in the first place.

The Truth is to realize that the only true flaw is believing you have flaws. You were never meant to be the version of perfect you think you must be. So let go of this fictious ideal version of you, and you'll be able to let go of the imperfections that you think you have.

As there are now no more benchmarks, you can allow in the thought that you are always perfect, because you were never meant to be any different or even any better than what you already are.

To say 'I need…' puts you on the path to be like others, but others do not see themselves as perfect, so this is a bit of a trap. Being like others is not honoring your individual perfection and will never lead to happiness.

Needing to be perfect is the void's need to fit in and hide itself in the world. The more perfect it is, the harder it is to spot. Stop feeding this need, and you will stop experiencing yourself as imperfect. Stand out instead, it is a celebration of your own uniqueness, something better than perfection.

"What is perfect about me, is that I can now see I was never all the things I thought made me imperfect. I was never the I, I thought I was."

People do not want what I have; they do not want me

Do you look at certain groups of people and decide that you will not fit in with them; that they will not want you, and you do not want them? We do this to protect ourselves, because we do not want to be hurt. We do not want to be made to feel different, unwanted, like a failure, or unloved. But whatever you bring with you into a space is what you are terrified will be shown up by others. You do not want to see your own issues and admit that you are the cause of not living your life to the fullest. You want everyone else to be the problem. It is you who doesn't not want what you have. You believe it makes you too different and an outcast. You have rejected yourself and you fear others will mirror this self-rejection to you.

You decided that what makes you different, makes you ugly, unwanted, undesirable and not special. Deciding not to want yourself has made you feel ugly, unwanted, undesirable and not special for yourself.

So, what is the Truth? Needing others to want you, over and above you wanting yourself, caused an emotional injury. You've since been hiding the real you, fearing you will one day feel rejected again. As a result, you have been holding yourself back for years—not to cause injury or harm, but to save yourself from injury and harm. Yet holding yourself back is the harm you have been worrying about most. Not wanting to see yourself is what caused the problem in the first place.

Decide that you are ready to see all of yourself, you welcome and embrace it. Forgive yourself for not being ready to see all your greatness until this moment.

"Seeing the real me is what the I has feared most."

I must criticize myself

Some of us are absolutely addicted to making ourselves wrong for virtually everything we do in life. We constantly criticize our every decision and keep punishing ourselves, no matter what. Everything we do is wrong or bad for some reason. This makes for a very stressful and unpleasant life.

Why do we do this?

We believe that to punish ourselves makes us a better person, that in some way it will improve our behavior and make us an optimal human being. The Truth is it is just perpetuating all those dysfunctional behaviors we are trying to get away from. Whatever we do not like about how we live just stays longer, the more we punish ourselves. We eat more, we love ourselves less, we are less loving and caring about others—all because we punish ourselves. It does not improve our behavior; it just worsens it.

If it does not do what we think it was meant to do, why do we do it?

Is it because we believe that is all we deserve? Is it because we think it is insurance against other people making us wrong for our entire life?

The Truth is, we are upset at ourselves for the first time we made a mistake. Not because we made a mistake but because we saw ourselves as

the mistake. We then hated that we labelled ourselves that way. We hated that we could define something as infinite and amazing as ourselves based on one tiny meaningless outcome. Then we hated that we hated ourselves. It has remained ever since.

Instead, we needed to congratulate ourselves for seeing our enormity in that split second, and how ludicrous it is to define something as infinite and amazing as ourselves based on any outcome. We are not the outcomes we experience in life and do not need to identify with them.

"I do not need labels for comfort or certainty; I can be certain no labels will ever describe my enormity."

I always need to doubt and question myself

For many of us growing up, there was always someone around to point out our mistakes. Our parents were there first and foremost, followed by our siblings, and then of course our teachers, who were often a bit trigger-happy with the red ink. Now as an adult, we fear being wrong, feeling rejected and being treated as an outcast.

But it was not all the criticism from others that made us feel this way; it was the criticism that came from ourselves. We sided with those who criticized us, agreeing with them. We decided we were not good enough and did not make the cut. That is what hurt us then, and still hurts us today.

The Truth is, doubting ourselves will not protect us from criticism, because it is a form of criticism. The best way to avoid being criticized or feeling criticized, is to not criticize ourselves. Realize that criticism will not help you prosper; being self-loving and nurturing will.

We did not need to buy into the Mindset all those years ago that it was necessary to be critical of ourselves. The smartest thing was to honor our strengths and find more things to love about ourselves, rather than more things we should have been better at.

Our biggest failure was allowing in the idea that failure is bad; and thinking that what we did was fail, so therefore we must be bad. We have

been critical of ourselves ever since, always trying to avoid concluding that we are bad and reliving the first time we decided we were bad.

What we really went through was believing we were bad for thinking we could ever be bad, and we have been nasty to ourselves ever since for having that thought.

"Being self-critical will not protect me from failure or criticism; self-love will. If I love what I do at the start, I will not have anything to criticize at the end."

"Believing I was an I, was the worst criticism I ever received, and the worst criticism I am still receiving."

I cannot be happy with myself

You may—even currently—experience people in your family as upsetting or frustrating, annoying or irritating. It is very easy to think that it is all about them; they just do not see eye to eye with you on things. You may even think that you cannot be happy with this person. But that thought is likely coming from the belief that you cannot be happy with yourself.

And yes, you originally learned this from a parent or guardian, or even a sibling. They decided they could not be happy with you—with themselves, of course, being at the heart of it all.

So, what is the Truth?

Trying to fit in with others, trying to please and impress others, has made us very unlikable to ourselves. What we fundamentally do not like is still trying to please others and be there for them in some way. The belief is that we need to be seen as helpful. It is time to be helpful to yourself, by no longer needing others to believe you are helpful.

We learned that not disappointing people is how we are liked and approved of. But to avoid disappointing others is the fastest way to not like or approve of ourselves. It is important to stand up for what our Truth is, even if it is unpopular, potentially disappointing, and even if there is a chance we will be seen as a letdown.

For many of us, feeling like a letdown is terrifying. But what had us feel this way in the first place is letting ourselves down by trying to please others. You cannot stop feeling like a letdown while you keep letting yourself down.

Deciding to be an I and then to put the I first was our first major let down.

"It is time to allow in what is best for me, and stop putting myself last to others and most importantly to the I. I cannot please the I. The more I try to please the I, the more unhappiness I experience."

I have a bad memory and forget a lot of things

Remembering the past is believed to be quite an achievement. Those that remember the most are held in high esteem, and therefore many of us aspire to be someone who has a great memory. The odd thing is that much of what we try to remember goes against creating the life we really desire for ourselves.

To have a great memory can often be a curse rather than a gift. Much of what you truly want to achieve requires you to forget your past rather than remember it. It is okay to have a less than ideal memory, because that means you are dragging around less of your past, making you far clearer to connect to your present and the inspiration from within.

The more your awareness must deal with matters of the past, the more you recreate your past in your future. Be grateful if your memory is less than ideal. As far as memories go, less is ideal. Now that you can stop punishing yourself for your memory not being as good as other people's, it will become sharper!

A great memory is not the secret to success or a great life; recognizing the Truth in each moment is. The past is gone, the future is made from the now, so all that is left is to know yourself in each moment.

You are not made from your past; believing this, keeps you stuck in reliving the past. You are not the mistakes of the past; the only mistake was thinking you are. You are not the regrets of the past; you are the genius that came forth in the spaces between the regrets. How you see yourself matters most of all. Are you being the mistakes or the regrets, or are you being the stillness and the love between them? The void regrets that it was never more than what it is. You do not need such regrets.

The most powerful inquiry you can make, is into who you are being right now. It shifts the focus from seeing yourself as the void, to seeing you as your whole, amazing, true self. If you want to remember something important, this is it!

"I do not need to remember the way (the) I was. The I wants to be remembered, the I is memory, but memory was never me."

I am a bad person

If I were to ask if you believe you are a bad person, your almost immediate response would most likely be 'absolutely not'. And that would be the correct answer, of course. But did you notice how you came to that answer? Were you aware of your reasons and justifications?

Did you catch yourself saying things about yourself, like being a nice, kind, giving, thoughtful person; that you do not steal or lie? What are you trying to cover up with all this? It is amazing how many reasons we can come up with to defend ourselves from thinking we are a bad person.

You may have noticed that you feel a bit uncertain about your answer. This is because despite all our reasons, all our justifications, and all our attempts in life to do the right thing and be a good person, we do believe deep down that we are a bad person.

Now, you might be immediately defending yourself, that this is not true; that you do not think you are a bad person. So let me delineate something for you. Thinking you are a bad person does not make you a bad person, nor is it an admission of guilt. But refusing to look deeply to see what

you really think about yourself keeps you believing you are a bad person. So be open to this introspection.

We have spent so much of our life trying to say the right thing, help where we can, give to charity, put ourselves last to please others, work hard, be seen as good—why? Is this because we do not actually believe we are bad? No, it is because we do already believe we are bad and are terrified to see it.

Being a bad person is terrifying for most of us, so we go to great lengths to avoid others feeling this way about us, and we go to even greater lengths to avoid feeling this way about ourselves.

The first realization required is that we never needed to decide whether we are good or bad, because that is where we become unstuck. We also need to realize that people are not looking at us, whether we are good or bad, to love us or not; only we are doing that to ourselves. The next realization is that we feel bad for labeling ourselves as bad, rather than for ever being bad. We feel even worse for forcing ourselves to be a person. We feel 'bad' for becoming a person, labelling ourselves this way, as an I.

Remember, the void loves labels! It is always attempting to define and classify something that is infinite—you—in very limited finite terms. Hence the identity.

Realize that you do not need to be good to love yourself, or receive love in this world. But believing you are everything that makes up your I is blocking your love right now. Love that you are realizing this now! Love yourself for this!

"The I is the person and I was never good at being that person, I was bad at it, and that is GREAT about me!"

I am not allowed to live the life I want

Many of us were stifled as children; we were forbidden to do what we really craved. We learned to believe that we are not allowed to do what we want,

nor have what we want in life. We also learned to believe that we must go without what we want; we must leave it behind and let it go; or the classic belief of not being able to have the nice things in life.

You can probably tell what destructive, sabotaging behaviors these beliefs set up for you. Try not to go there, though.

So, what is the Truth? The irony is that you are living the life you want. It may not be the most ideal version of what you want, but it is the life you want right here, right now. It is not really the life you want to experience, but it is the only life you will allow in.

The life you really want to experience is the life you will not allow in just yet owing a lot to this belief. This belief is tricky because it disempowers you; it makes you seem more like a victim than the cause and creator of your life.

We get annoyed because we are trapping ourselves in a life that we accept, but do not want. The reason is that it is our Mind's life we are living, and deep down we know it is not the life we were meant for. So, the Mind is allowed to create and experience this life, but we cannot have the real life that is possible.

This is because we cannot accept things that are too good. We reject them; we are suspicious of them. Remember, if something conflicts or contradicts your identity—what you have imagined for yourself and as yourself—you will struggle to let it into your reality.

Behind this is a very hidden and secret belief that if we have a great life, our Mind will cease to exist; we will not get all the things we think matter to our identity. This is seen as a loss of control. And we do not want to be out of control, for better or for worse. We believe being out of control means to fail, to go without.

So, we are trapped in not just a life we settle for, but in the need to maintain control. Control is what suffocates and stifles us—control over us as kids, and now the need for control as adults. This is a big one to let

in: Let go of needing control, and you will have the life you really want. Realize that you are the one not allowing yourself to live the life you really want, because you believe living out all your beliefs is more important to you.

The Truth is to see that needing life to be any different is not coming from a place of power, but from self-rejection. It means you have failed in some way to improve life. This is not self-belief, and self-belief is what is required to manifest new experiences.

Rather, see life as a perfect manifestation of where you are, a direct result of holding onto the beliefs you still have. Your life is not a product of failure. If you want a new reality, you must seek a new expanded identity, or be free from it completely.

It is time to let go of what has been holding you back. Let go of the beliefs around needing to suffer first, before experiencing rapid growth and change. Change can be quick and painless if you let go of needing to fail as part of the process.

"I cannot have the life I want while needing to keep the identity I have. That identity was not me or a person, but a collection of beliefs that thought they were way more important than the real me. "

This brings us to a new awareness – thoughts have the capacity to think. All this time we believed we were the thinkers. It's more accurate to say we have been aware of what our thoughts think of themselves, and we have experienced that as what we think of ourselves.

"Thoughts think of themselves, but I was never the deficit they see themselves as."

I am my thoughts

Spring boarding off that, one of the hardest things about being alive is the illusion that we are our thoughts. Identifying with our thoughts is limiting and painful.

We were never told that we were not our thoughts, so we have just assumed that is the substance from which we are made. But thoughts are not what we think or believe they are. And here is the jaw-dropper: Your thoughts do not belong to you. In fact, all thoughts exist outside of you, like frequencies floating in the air. You draw on them, use them to give you different perspectives and experiences, but they are not you or from you. When thoughts are bundled together and seen as what you are, they create a Mind, "your Mind".

Sure, you have adopted them as your own, and worst of all, you have identified with them as if they are your intrinsic DNA. Think of thoughts like a fungus; they grow where it is dark and damp. They are not a product of Enlightenment but rather exist right up until enlightenment.

What does this mean for you? Stop engaging with thoughts. Stop needing them to busy yourself. Stop going over old thoughts. And stop seeing thoughts as the path to clarity or understanding; see them instead as the obstacle to clarity and understanding. Thoughts are not you!

The belief is that we need thoughts to be ourselves, but the Truth is that when we are without thoughts, the real us will emerge. We are the space and clarity between thoughts. Thoughts are the Mind's commentary. Thoughts are the voice of the void. In the absence of thought is stillness and love; this is the real you.

You think you need thoughts to light your path, but thoughts cast doubt over it instead. You believe thoughts help you to see reason and logic but knowing does that even faster. Thoughts are not your consciousness; they only hide your true consciousness and infinite intelligence from you. The Mind is made-up and so are the thoughts it has.

"I am the Truth that remains in the silence and stillness of the Mind, infinity without questions."

I have more to go, more to do, before I can be happy with myself

As children we learn what it takes to get noticed. We can scream and throw tantrums, injure ourselves, or we can be more impressive than anyone else. For many of us, being impressive was the only real way to stand out from the crowd and be seen as a somebody.

The unfortunate thing about this strategy is that many of us are still drawing upon it today as adults. We never learned to let it go, so even today we believe we must keep going the extra mile, doing more, and being impressive so we get the desired attention we are after.

If you are trying to be noticed out there in the world, it is important to look at how you really feel about yourself. Are you trying to be noticed to earn more money, achieve a new title, increase opportunities in your life—or are you determined to finally get the recognition you have always sought from yourself?

When will enough be enough? When will you be enough to recognize yourself, is the question. We achieve greatness in our lives and fail to see it because enough is never enough. Why? Because we look at the failures rather than the wins, the disappointments rather than the accomplishments. We live with regret over the milestones won. But what is behind this self-destructive way of being? We identified with the belief that we will never be enough. While you believe you are only a belief, you cannot ever feel enough. It is simply not enough to see yourself as a belief.

We could relate to ourselves as the perfection that is the human body, it's amazing inner workings and the ever-providing Universe. Instead, we relate to ourselves as the fragile Mind occupying the body. And this is what sees itself as never being enough. The Mind believes it will never be enough, and it is correct. We on the other hand were never made of the thought 'I will never be enough' but it will be how we see ourselves if we insist on identifying with the I. Realize we are not the I that believes it's not enough.

"I am that which has provided enough; I am that which enables all bodies to perform and deliver all that is required of them. I have already given enough. I am the substance that makes life possible—not the substance that keeps questioning life."

I do not want to be enough

There is a significant fear preventing us from ever feeling enough: If we ever become enough, we will suffer for it.

Some of us were shut down whenever we displayed any greatness or talent; we were yelled at or criticized for being a show-off. Others learned that the greater we are, the less appealing we are to those around us. We watched others switch off their love for us because of it, and so we learned to switch off our own love for ourselves.

This is the most worrying fear of all for us, that if we become enough, we will not actually love ourselves or give ourselves any love. We learn to modify or water down our greatness, as it brings unpleasant experiences.

The Truth is, it is not our greatness that ever harmed us, but rather switching off our love for ourselves and failing to love ourselves. We learned to mimic those around us, and as soon as we switched on our greatness, we learned to switch off our love. Greatness is not what harmed us; it was believing we were something else, something less: the Minds opinion of our greatness.

Keep giving yourself love for all acts of your greatness, and you will not switch off your greatness or your love. If you give yourself love for your greatness, you will always succeed in life.

"If I stop seeing myself as the I and all its opinions of me, I will find all the greatness and the love I have been searching for."

I am always wrong; none of my ideas work out or get me anywhere

When you are shut down a lot as a child—which inevitably happens—your ideas do not get heard, or people show no real interest in them, it

is easy to get disheartened. But no one with great ideas was ever heard by common Minds. Common Minds avoid greatness at all costs, as it shows them up for settling for mediocrity within themselves. It shows them up for never believing in themselves and what they have to offer…and that is difficult to take from a child.

Ideas are magical; they have the power to change your life and the lives of others if they are not squashed in the early days. Ideas need time to become strong on their own. Unfortunately, many geniuses have been put off ever celebrating and feeling the benefits of their greatness because they put too much stock in mediocre Minds. That's what you did many years ago when you began adopting your identity. You put too much stock in the Mind itself, rather than believing in the idea that is the REAL you. You chose to be the I instead. You gave up on something priceless for something worthless, and you have never recovered from it.

This behavior has carried forward so now it is not your ideas you worry about failing; it is your belief in yourself. You worry that you will fail to believe in yourself at the critical moments, the same as what you did all those years ago.

You can see now that everything that we fear, everything that shows up as present day concerns began years ago as early as our first thoughts. The damage was done then at the time we substituted our truth for the Mind's lies, when we took on the I as our true self.

Stand behind your greatness. You are safe with all your ideas. Your ideas are your essence; they are everything you are: limitless ideas. Connecting back to that and believing in your own ideas is the safest place on Earth. Your ideas are for you, and they only need to matter to you first before they can possibly mater to anybody else.

"I am the best idea the Universe has ever had! My ideas are the Universe's ideas."

I don't see myself as great

Let us begin this one by starting with the most important question: Why are we so reluctant to see ourselves as great? Why do we filter out self-love wherever possible?

It is because we believe we are still not perfect. We believe we have issues because we are not perfect yet. We get angry, frustrated, fearful, antagonistic, withdrawn, held back, irritable, and so on. We think if we still possess all these undesirable qualities, then how can we call ourselves perfect? And how on Earth could we possibly love ourselves for having all these issues?

Realize that the self we believe has all these shortcomings was never real in the first place. The precise reason you are still experiencing shortcomings is because you believe yourself to be this self, and you believe this self to be full of issues.

The Truth is, it is not your journey to get perfect or even be rid of your undesirable traits or qualities. That pursuit keeps you perceiving yourself as imperfect your entire life. The Mind does not see itself as perfect, the Mind does not love itself, it believes it is underserving of love. We experience these as our thoughts because we believe we are the Mind.

You will experience yourself as whatever you believe you are.

"It's perfect to have the choice to either see myself as the emptiness that is the Mind and experience what it experiences or to see myself as the perfection that created this choice."

Everyone else knows better than me

Many of us are worried that we will never know the best way to live, and we think that everyone else has figured it out. We fear we will keep getting it wrong and keep creating unpleasant experiences in our life. We think there is an ideal way to spend our day, but it is a secret, and we will never get to discover it.

Interestingly, this belief is not about the best way to live your day or even how to make the most of your day; it is the worry that you have already made the least of your life. You fear that every decision you have made so far has been wrong, appalling, and you have let yourself down every step of the way. You worry that you are poor at decision making, and you think there are always better decisions to make, but these are always elusive to you.

Realize that life is not about making the best decisions possible in every moment, because that creates pressure and stress. It is not the decisions we make that create a better life; it is the love we give ourselves prior to making a decision that creates a better life.

We constantly tell ourselves that we need to strive for more, to plan our future so it is better than the past and present. We reject the present in exchange for making a better tomorrow. In doing so, we deprive ourselves of love before making any decisions and then wonder why all our decisions keep leading to virtually the same quality of experiences.

We see so many fortunate people who seem to have been given more than us; at earlier ages they were given a leg up for easier and sweeter victories. What we do not see is our divinity. Instead, we feel we are running out of chances to make this a great life, so we think we must hurry before we get too old and this window closes, and our life remains forever dull and boring.

So, what is the Truth? First, recognize that the problem lies in how you assess your life thus far. It is in the judgment that you have created a problem for yourself. If you have never had a benchmark with which to compare your life, you would be without judgment and with total acceptance.

Your life has not been squandered. You cannot imagine how much worse it could have been, how much worse it could have turned out. We worry about missed opportunities and poor decisions. But the decisions you made were the best you could make in each moment.

Thank yourself for not squandering your life. You have always strived for more, which means you never squandered your life. You have just been learning that self-love makes for better decisions than the need to get life right. Make decisions from a space of self-love rather than from a space of getting it wrong again, and great decisions, made effortlessly, will follow.

What we have squandered is not life or our decisions, but the opportunities to give ourselves love. This is what hurts. In fact we have squandered our chance to see ourselves as Love by choosing to instead see ourselves as the I. This shows us the actual decision we regret most, our earliest decision, which is deciding to be the Mind, that to be like others is better than being the Love that we are. We believed everyone else knows better than me, so we chose what they chose, we chose to be the Mind over our True-Self. We have regretted this decision ever since and so whenever decisions arise, we fear they too will be regretted.

We regret missing out on our love in the hope the Mind could offer us more. But we were always more before the Mind, we were Love. Love is infinite, love is eternal, love is our very essence and therefore the opposite of the Mind. The Mind is emptiness, neediness, a void full of FEAR.

"The quality of my decisions does not define the quantity of how much love I can allow for myself, but the quantity of the love I have for myself prior to making a decision will dictate the quality of the outcomes I create."

I have to make others happy

We have been taught that the more we please others, the more love and attention we get and the better we get to feel about ourselves. We have also been taught that the more we help and support others, the more we find ourselves in their good graces. This is what Mom and Dad taught us.

This is how the world works. We help others; we get liked. But where that leaves us is building our entire life around being there for others, pleasing others, getting their attention, doing great things for them, relieving their pain, showing up as their hero, and what is worse, sidelining ourselves just to please everyone else.

After all, how else are we going to love ourselves? We believe that the more we please others, the more they will like and approve of us, and therefore the more we will like and approve of ourselves. We feel that helping the world is a good deed, and the greater the number of good deeds that we do, the more we like ourselves.

The trouble is, the more we do for the world, inadvertently leaving ourselves out of the equation, the less we really do like ourselves. Self-love does not come from doing good deeds for others. It comes from doing good deeds for yourself. In fact, we hate to be ignored or sidelined by ourselves. We hate coming in last to others; we hate having our fun taken away in pursuit of approval from others. We hate self-deprivation in pursuit of the elusive self-love. Why? Because it's what we did to ourselves all those years ago.

One of earliest choices in life was "I need to become an I to please others." and because we believe we need to please others we therefore believe we must keep being an I. Talk about sidelining ourselves! We did it back then and so we are still doing it now.

"There are no others to please, just more I's. Pleasing the I's in the world will never please me."

I have to be of service

As children, we are taught that we are not being good human beings if we are not helping Mom and Dad in the house. And to further that, we must also immediately offer to help. We are told to help the elderly with their groceries, and the needy through charities.

We are taught to get a job and help whenever and wherever we can, or we will not get paid. We are also taught that our life purpose on this Earth is to be of service to others, to give if we want to receive, and to keep giving throughout our life.

The problem with all of this is the emphasis on giving and not receiving. This sets us up to make our own life about everyone else and what they

need, rather than about what we need in our own life. This can easily turn into a subconscious pattern that means we cannot even imagine coming in anything other than last—and we must give to others first and foremost.

This becomes exhausting and depressing because we starve ourselves of the joy, love, and attention we need to grow and heal.

It is interesting how the Mind has executed all of this so perfectly. It reassures us that our fulfillment comes externally from helping others and that to think of ourselves first, is selfish. But as we put our needs last, something begins to go horribly wrong. We become discontent, full of regret for how we have spent our life. We have disdain for our efforts and for how we have spent our time.

The result is that the Mind is in full control, with regret as its motto. So, if you are experiencing a lot of regret in your life, it is likely because you have spent your life trying to please others, while putting your own needs last.

So, what is the Truth? To give to yourself is one of the highest acts in the Universe. To give through love, admiration, appreciation, and recognition of your own greatness is what the Universe aspires for us all. Without this to balance giving to others, regret is inevitable.

If you are going to give to others, you must be in recognition of your greatness throughout. You cannot wait until the very end of your life to congratulate yourself. You cannot deprive yourself of the respect you deserve for all that you have done. It must be a now sentiment.

Where this need originated from was when we gave up giving to ourselves. As soon as we chose to see ourselves as the I, as the Mind instead of seeing ourselves as Love, we stopped being of service to ourselves. We took so much from ourselves that we have been trying to compensate for that ever since. The I believes that to be of service to everybody else would be a great substitute for failing to be of service to ourselves. It thinks by giving to everyone else we can replace what we took from ourselves all those years ago. Of course, this incorrect.

"Being me is the greatest gift to myself I can ever give. It is also the greatest gift I can give to everyone else who are still trying to wake up from being an I. By shinning my greatness others will learn how to do the same."

My life can only begin when I am truly successful

Do you ever find yourself waiting for an event to happen: a pay rise, a huge influx of cash, or a new level of recognition? Are you waiting for success to arrive before you will allow yourself to start living? What is it you are really waiting for? Because it is certainly not what it seems.

We think we are waiting for success before we push the live button—or have we had our finger on the die button all this time? We have been taught life is not worth living unless we have lots of money, unless we are a recognized somebody, unless we are free to do whatever we want whenever we want, but what is the Truth? We are wasting our life waiting for any of these things.

What if success is happening right now? You would not even notice it.

Success is occurring at a far deeper level than you allow yourself to be present to. Today is the success over yesterday. This month is the success you wanted six months ago. This year is the success you wanted ten years ago. Success is your inherit being, hidden underneath the thoughts "I am…"

You cannot see it, of course; you are too busy looking way out in front of you, waiting for the future successes to arrive. Success does not arrive in your future; it comes in your present. If you are looking in your future, you will miss what is given in your present. Success is a moment-to-moment realization, from one triumphant moment to the next.

This experience of being without success originated very early on when we decided that what I am, is not enough to succeed in this life-time. What we were hoping for was the biggest success imaginable and that was to remain as our True-Self and not follow the footsteps of others losing our True-Self for the Mind. That's the biggest success the Universe can hope

for, is that each soul can maintain their view of themselves throughout birth and childhood into their adult years. We believe we were unsuccessful in believing in ourselves enough to keep the identity at bay. So, whenever the opportunity arises to see ourselves as our Truth or as the Mind we fear we will do it all again. This becomes a constant reMinder that we are unsuccessful.

"I am not the times I believe I am the identity I am the success that remains constant despite the identity."

I regret everything I do

Some of us can really celebrate what we do in life, while the rest of us constantly question and even regret everything we do. What are we getting from this that we keep torturing ourselves this way? We only torture ourselves if we believe we are getting something out of it.

We think questioning ourselves and even regretting something is a way to avoid making a future mistake. If we catch ourselves early on, we think, we can turn a mistake around and make it a success instead. But the cost of always questioning takes away the upside of the success.

We need to see what we are really striving for here. It is not to avoid making a mistake; it is to avoid always seeing ourselves as someone who gets everything wrong no matter how hard we try.

This highlights the multifaceted non-truth that our job in life is to seize every moment, take advantage of every opportunity, never fail at anything at all, and always be victorious at every possible turn. In other words, we actually believe that we always lose. Because of this belief, we just expect to get everything wrong. It is torturous to believe that no matter how hard we try, no matter how smart we are, we cannot live our greatness because we see ourselves as someone who always loses. This gives rise to jealousy because it looks like everyone else can win and get things right except for us—a very painful belief!

So, what is the healing Truth? We are not here to try to get everything right; we are not here to win; we are here to see that we never needed to try in the first place. You cannot win at everything or get everything right. But you can realize that not trying to win at everything, not trying to get everything right, creates a much more successful life than the alternative.

It is time to see that what had us feeling so very wrong was trying so hard to be who we believed everyone expected us to be. Guess who this was? That's right, the Mind, the I. We secretly know trying to be the best I possible is impossible! You can't be an I and you certainly can't be the best I, because they are a different substance to what you actually are. The identity is made up, but you are real. So trying to be something that isn't real is doomed to failure right from the onset. In Truth, our expectation that we could ever be an I and even a great I was one of earliest failings. In that moment we experienced huge regret. And worse we decided we were this regret that we felt. Because we felt regret, we decided "I am regret."

This brings up a new level of awakening, of believing we are what we feel like. From the earliest age we began to feel things inside of ourselves and we began to identify ourselves with these feelings. We decided if I feel it, it must be me. This is of course not the truth. What we identified with was not what WE felt like but what thoughts and beliefs felt like in the body. There is no identity in what we really feel like, just an identity in what thoughts and beliefs feel like. In this instance we felt 'regret' within us and we chose to identify with that sensation. We continued to do this with countless other sensations in the body choosing to label ourselves as that sensation.

We even do it today – people ask how are you feeling today, and we take that to mean what I feel inside of me is what I feel like. We answer describing what we feel like but in truth, we describe what the I feels like. Instead, people should be asking, "WHAT are you feeling today?".

"What I regret the most is seeing myself as the regret I felt when I decided I could be a great I. Needing to be my feelings was unnecessary."

I fear I will run out and be left with nothing

Do you worry about not having enough food or money? Do you find you obsess about how to keep more coming in? This comes from having things taken away from you as a child, and not only that, from getting scorned for running out and not having anything left. It could have been finishing your candy too quickly, losing a brand-new toy, or giving a friend something, Mom or Dad cherished and had given you.

Of course, now it is often about running out of money, having spent it too quickly, and getting into trouble for that. This is the worry or fear that you will never get it back because that is the message you received as a child. You were told that you have lost it or run out, so you will not get any more. And maybe you were also punished for that, so now as an adult you must punish yourself.

On a deeper level, the fear is that you will hate yourself for it. You will regret losing what is of value because you will be so mean to yourself that you will not even like yourself because of it.

How do you mend this fear? Recognize that the first time you scorned yourself was not for running out of something or having less, but from believing in that moment you were less because of it. To say you are less is what is excruciating—far worse than running out of something that can be gotten again.

So what was this originating moment where we went from seeing ourselves as infinite beings to deciding we are so much less than that?

It occurred when we first felt what being an I and "having" a Mind actually felt like. It was less, it felt less, and we confused these feelings of less for what our true nature felt like. We decided "I am these feelings, I am less", that's what I am. Once again, we mistook what thoughts and beliefs feel like for what we feel like. One thing was clear they feel a lot less than what we knew to be our true-self.

The truth of course is that you are limitless. You are an endless reservoir of everything you will ever need. And yes, you have seen people run out of money and never get it back, but that is because they do not see themselves as limitless. But you can return to this view of yourself, and so you can keep creating more and more.

It is having less or having none that is not you; having more is the true you. More is what comes naturally, but less was never you in the first place. You are more of everything, so you can experience more of everything.

"Less is how the I sees itself. I am not this 'less' To see myself as feelings is me being much less."

I cannot get life to work for me; things never go my way

Do you feel that you are constantly up against life? That what you want will inevitably be a fight against life and ultimately will never work out? After experiencing many failures as a child and much opposition from parents, many of us end up believing that life simply does not work out for us.

And so, the questions arise as to why we bother trying so hard in the first place? Why so we bother wanting anything outside the norm? Ironically, it is so we can prove that life does not work out for us.

We have become prone to wanting or desiring things outside of our flow. It is not that life does not want to give to you—on the contrary, that is all life wants. It is you who has stopped wanting to give to you. At some point, you decided to take from yourself. And from that point on, many of your ideas became detrimental.

This is why so many of your ideas seem doomed to fail from the start. The secret is, you do not realize that you are trying to take from yourself when you think you are trying to give to yourself. So many ideas you have would really hurt you if they did come to fruition.

Let us clear the need to take from ourselves so we can start giving to ourselves. The need to take from ourselves arose when we believed we were

not as good as everyone else. From that point on, we believed we needed to compete with everybody else. This began the taking.

What we need to realize instead, is that everybody is already taking from themselves. If we try to be like them, we will be taking from ourselves. If we follow them, try to be like them, want what they want, strive like they strive, need like they need, we will forever take from ourselves.

What is really taking from us is the belief that we need to see ourselves like others. The more we do what they do, the more life lets us know that we are not like them, so life will not give us what they have. Life wants to give us what is meant only for us.

So, the Truth is, it is not life that is against you; it is you who is against living your own life.

Why fight what is specifically for you in this lifetime? It is because you were taught to beat life—to win against life rather than flow with it. Only the strong will prosper, only the persistent will succeed, and so on. While some of this is true, you must be pointing in the right direction for these cliches to apply.

The right direction is not facing outward and seeing your competition, but rather facing inward where your heart wants to go. It is not conquering that is required; it is listening. It is not force that is required; it is fearlessness. It is the realization that if you follow the path chosen for you, then and only then will you truly succeed.

Let's face it, the moment we decided we need to be an I to have and experience what everyone else has, life became a struggle. We left the reason why we came to this Earth, and we made life about someone else's reason for coming to this Earth. How else could life go after that? It's like a Train jumping off its train racks to try to be a boat. Well, we all know how that would end. Trying to be an I is difficult but trying to be a different I and be same I as others is more than double the challenge.

"Nobody else's path is meant for me. My path is what is meant for me. My I does not know the best path for me because it thinks everyone else's path is best for me. Love is the best path, being Love is my path."

If I do not think things through, I will slip up

Many of us continually think about things, even when we are not aware of it. We find it hard to shut off our thinking, even when on the surface there appears to be no rhyme or reason to it. We have a program running that keeps our thinking brain working around the clock.

We believe it is ensuring our safety when it is really robbing us of our freedom and relaxation. We are taught to think before we leap, to plan ahead and be certain before we make decisions. All this very unhelpful parental advice has built us into thinking—not resting—machines.

We now believe that thinking, not the absence of thinking, is our insurance policy against failure and miscalculation. And it is hard to argue with this. We have come to see thinking to mean seeing all the variables, outcomes, and different pathways. But have we ever seen those other pathways?

So, what is the Truth? There is none, at least not about thinking. It is a pointless exercise that wears you down, tires your brain and body, and leaves you more confused than when you began. The trouble started when you believed you were in danger in the first place.

You see, it was not the thinking or even the non-thinking that caused the problem; it was believing that life is full of pitfalls you will inevitably fall into. We were taught that life is hazardous and if we do not look before we leap, we can pretty much guarantee that we are doomed. Is life that treacherous? Are we really doomed?

The Truth is, telling you that life is treacherous is what made it treacherous for you. You expect it, so you create it. But what if you realized something different? What if you realized that life just wanted to keep giving to you? Life already gave to you—it birthed you into this world and has been

fighting for you ever since. It has put air into your lungs, food into your gut, oceans to cleanse your body and Mind, and continually brings wisdom through life experiences and direct connection to itself.

Why discount all life gives and believe that all it does is take away? Why believe what everybody else wants to believe?

The Truth is, we do not want to see how much life gives because we desperately want to believe we are strong against life, a force to be reckoned with all on our own. We all know that when life wants to exert its power, no human being is any match.

The more we flow with life, the more we prosper. Recognizing its bounty and generosity is the first step to creating flow and momentum. See how much life wants to give to you by realizing how much you have already got.

It is not through thinking that you avoid life's pitfalls, but by realizing there were never any pitfalls in the first place, because life cannot help but keep giving to you.

The essence of this dilemma is that we identified with having thoughts as our true nature. The more thoughts we had, the harder it became to see the life-giving nature of life itself. Thoughts became the distraction and deteriorated our ability to see the most powerful Truth there is: We are life, giving to ourselves.

Instead, we saw that we are thought thinking beings, being buffeted by life. But it is having thoughts and worse, identifying with these thoughts, that buffets us around in life. To see ourselves as life itself is the fastest, most direct access to having flow in life. You see, the less we see ourselves as life, the more we slip up; the more we see ourselves as life, the more effortless being alive is for us.

"If I am open to receiving, I do not need to be thinking."

"Being open to more thinking closes me off from more receiving. I receive more when I think less."

"Life just wants me to see myself as Life, not as any other lesser idea of myself."

I need to spend lots of money to feel successful

Many of us get ourselves into a position where what we really want—or at least what we believe we want—is just out of our reach. What we deem as fun is often way too expensive for us. As a result, we become miserable because we feel we cannot afford to have any real fun.

We then feel constantly let down and feel that we cannot afford what we want. The pattern, of course, is subjecting ourselves to wanting what we cannot have and then experiencing misery. This leads to feeling like a constant failure and feeling that life is a constant letdown.

So why do we gravitate toward what we cannot afford? To feel like a failure? To feel that life is against us? Why would we want this? To prove a point—that we are hard done by, and no one really cares about us or thinks we are worth spending money on.

We decided as children to test how valuable we are—or how valuable we are not—so we got our parents and caregivers to often spend more than they had. This was our way of feeling somewhat accomplished and even loved.

Now as adults, we are doing this to ourselves, thinking that if we give ourselves more than we can afford, it means we have achieved greatly. The Truth we do not want to see is that we are the ones that are making ourselves feel unvalued and like a failure in the first place.

If we did not need to do more to feel like more, we would feel okay within ourselves. So, it all comes down to thinking that spending more means we are more; doing more means we are more. But there is a subtlety underneath it all, which is the belief that we must always see our worth.

We came to believe that we always need to feel valued, important, loved, cherished, and the most valuable thing in everyone's life. That was

because we accepted that any ideas of being valuable and worthwhile did not aptly describe us, and so we strived for these things.

But what was not valuable or worthwhile was the idea that we must find our worth. And instead of this leading us to feel good about ourselves, it has led us on a wild goose chase our whole life.

Instead, we are meant to realize that we cannot find our value and worth in words, or in other people, but in how we define ourselves. The most valuable thing we could have ever done was to not have tried to define ourselves to find value. Defining oneself excludes value; it is not a worthwhile thing to do.

We decided we needed definition to find our value. And in that moment, it became impossible to see our value, and the need to find our value became intense. The Mind seeks to value itself using material means, labels and definitions. It is trying to make itself real. The more real it appears the more we believe in it as who we are.

The trouble began when years ago, we attempted to find our value, to look for it, and we couldn't find it. We mistook not finding our value for not having any value. The reason we couldn't find it is because it is beyond measure, beyond definition. Our value is limitless.

Instead of seeing our infinite nature as our value we decided to see ourselves as the emptiness that exists between looking for value and not finding it. We decided we are that which has no value.

This brings up another level of awareness. Not only have we identified with thoughts, beliefs and feelings but here we are identifying with what's perceived as missing, as 'needs' themselves. This is the very nature of the Mind, always needing, always being without. Become present to how many needs you believe you have because these are the needs you believe you are.

"I am not the search for value, nor the need for value, that is the I, not me".

"Giving into the idea that something only has worth if it can be defined or measured was not my idea but the Mind's idea. The real me was not the space where something is missing, the real me is the space that birthed EVERYTHING."

I am dull and boring

Many of us reach a point in our relationships and careers when we feel the need to break free. We desire a more exciting, adventurous, stimulating, and interesting life. But what is at the heart of this is something that has been in your life a very long time: you.

You have become bored with yourself—or more accurately stated, you are now aware that you feel bored and dull with yourself. You decided years ago that life is dull and boring being you, and ever since you have been trying to fill your life with thrills and adventure. As soon as you sit still long enough, you begin to feel bored and even depressed. This belief creates a lot of change in your life and does not support your long-term path.

So, what is the Truth? Realize that it is not you who needs fixing—it is the idea you have about yourself.

Constantly having inaccurate ideas about yourself is dull and boring to you. These include ideas such as needing to get along with others; needing to be more like others; needing to be more interesting; and believing that other people find you boring.

You never needed to be bored with yourself just because you are not like other people. You also do not need to be busy with projects all the time, so you will not feel bored and uninteresting. But you do need to stop being affected by the idea that you are dull and boring. Realize that it is dull and boring to keep having to change your life.

It is not recognizing your greatness that makes you feel the most bored and the most uninteresting. When you were young, you believed that everyone else had more than you. So, you stopped looking at what you have that shines. This is why you are bored.

You decided that everyone else is content with their greatness, but I want to be more like everyone else. In your head, this was not you being great, but you being weak and uninteresting. The Truth is that focusing more on what makes others great and less on what makes you great gets boring very quickly.

Where this originated from is identifying with something we saw missing. We couldn't see ourselves, so the thought we identified with was "I should be able to see more in myself". This led us up the proverbial garden path looking for ourselves everywhere but where we exist. We are still doing this today.

The Mind can't imagine or quantify something as vast and infinite as we truly are. It refuses to accept something that is beyond measure or physical definition. Because we couldn't see ourselves, we gave up on looking, deciding there isn't enough of ourselves to see. This decision was immensely painful of course, and is a major reason we don't want to sit still with ourselves because what happened the last time we did.

This "giving up" on trying to see or find the true-self meant we would make up a false self, through identifying with things, thoughts, feelings and gaps to fill in the picture of what makes us. We learnt to stop looking for our true-self early on leading to feelings of restlessness, boredom and discontentment.

All of which drives us to keep busy trying to find ourselves in others, in what we do, in what we create, in what we think, in how others see us and so on.

The Truth of course is "Being me is the most interesting thing there is. Just because the I can't see me, doesn't mean there is no Me. When you are EVERYTHING the Mind can't see where you begin and where you end."

You're Doing Great!

Congratulations! You've already moved mountains on your Losing Your Mind journey, taking quantum leaps in your growth!

As we are about to go even deeper, it is a perfect time to remind you about the **EnlightenMe Machine**....

- Go Beyond The Mind Into Your True-Self
- Clear Out Years of Beliefs, Anger and Resentment
- Become Open to Forgiveness and Emotional Healing
- **PLUS** 48 Weeks Online Training and Clearing with Daniel

Order Yours Now!

www.EnlightenMe.today

I have to stick to my Identity

People spend their entire lives trying to break the mold they have imprisoned themselves in, looking for dramatic ways to be different, radical, unconventional. There is an urge to become free in an explosive way to feel liberated and expansive. This often leads to wanting to break out of relationships, careers, and healthy behaviors. But it is not just situations we seek to be free from; it is wanting to break out and be free from our own Mind. The feeling is that we hate being trapped inside of being ourselves and needing a release.

The Truth has many layers. You are not trapped inside being you. You were never this you. You never liked being this you because it was never you in the first place. We began to feel stuck when we believed that we must think what we think, stand by what we believe, because all of this is what makes us who we are.

We decided that our thoughts are who we are, so we should stick with them; in other words, we are stuck with them. We also believed that we are stuck being who people think we are, and we are stuck believing in that too.

Now it is time to go to a deeper a level, where we get to understand the true nature of thought as we have spent our whole life with a huge misunderstanding.

The belief 'I am stuck' is referring to the thought itself 'I am stuck'. The thought believes it is stuck; we are not stuck. This brings us to an EMORMOUS realization: Thoughts describe themselves, they do not describe you!

Thoughts are the experiences they describe. The thought of being stuck is the thought experiencing itself as being stuck.

Thoughts are more than just fleeting experiences in our consciousness. A thought is a **conscious substance unto itself,** experiencing itself as the very energy it is about.

When we identify with a thought, we see ourselves as the thought, we then experience ourselves as the very essence and meaning of that thought.

Imagine it like this: the thought 'I am stuck' is the thought talking about itself. It believes it is stuck and this thought carries the energy or sensation of what it feels like to be stuck.

We were never what was stuck; only the thought was stuck. We are boundless, expansive, everywhere, and everything all at once.

"You are that which sees the thoughts, but you are not the thoughts or the experience they are having for themselves, unless you choose that for yourself."

I cannot allow success

Easily one of the biggest obstacles in the way of achieving success in life and even seeing how successful we already are, is the fear of success itself. We often think fear of failure is the major blockage, but fear of success is what is really behind us holding ourselves back.

But what is there to fear about success, you may ask? Surprisingly, what success has come to mean is now quite terrifying, more than you would think. We have a lot of fear around what will become of us if success takes hold. We imagine all kinds of retribution, financial assaults, insults, attacks, and worse. We have been told that people attack, criticize, sue, and con the successful, and we have even been told people change when they become successful. We have built having success as a detrimental thing.

The Truth is, it is not about how others see us that worries us—it is about whether we can get there and stay there with a clear conscience. Many of us worry that we will join the ranks of other wealthy people who have trodden over others or sold their souls to get to a better financial position in life.

We worry what we will think of ourselves if we become truly successful. Will we stop caring about our health, our loved ones, the Earth? Will we

lose sight of why we began this journey in the first place? Will we end up on drugs or with other addictions? Who will we become?

Interestingly, what we are afraid of is the person we imagined we would be all those years ago, when we first decided we need to be successful. We made up a person, a lifestyle, what would become available to us, how we would act, and where we would live. This person we made up that had us attracted to being successful in the first place is what we are really afraid of.

It could be based on a movie star or character in a film, a business-person, a world leader, or someone you knew growing up. Whoever you imagined yourself to be when successful is what you now fear, so you subconsciously apply the brakes moving forward.

The Truth is true success is not needing to be this person or be like anyone you have conjured up in your imagination. Realize that the person you made up is not the definition of success, but rather success gone horribly wrong.

Being successful is simply you being yourself, with greater means to share the love you have with others and the planet. The belief hiding here is that you cannot be successful because you cannot be the way you have seen successful people be; it will not work in your life.

The Truth is that success does not take acquiring more than you have right now; it takes seeing that you were never less than these people in the first place. You just decided you were.

Believing you needed what others had, to be happy and content made you see yourself as less than. Believing that you need success and that you are nothing without it, made you feel empty without it.

The thought 'I cannot allow success' is not about you and never was. It is the thought that cannot allow success, not you. Disassociate yourself from needing to identify as the thought itself. It cannot allow success, but you can. Realizing you are not this thought, is you being a SUCCESS!

You are afraid that you would be nothing if you don't create success. The truth is the emptiness you fear you already are is in fact the EVERYTHING you never let yourself see. As nothing you are everything, and you therefore need nothing.

I do not know enough

It is easy to believe we do not know enough when early on as children we get told that we should have known better. Then at school we were quizzed to see how much or how little we know to the point of being graded on how much we know.

We grow up and compare ourselves to the smartest people around us, often feeling inadequate that we know less. What is worse, we live in a society that believes the more you know, the more successful and fulfilled your life will be. And then it becomes a constant nagging thought in the background never leaving us alone, that we do not know enough, often cutting us down and leaving us feeling that we do not have what it takes to have a great life.

So, what is the Truth? We decided early on that the thoughts we have are not enough. We need more thoughts. After all, knowing more is simply having more thoughts than we had before. As we decided that we need to know more, a new thought was added into the Mind: 'I need more thoughts.' As we adopted this thought as one of our own, we took on its identity. We began to live that very experience and began feeling as though we need more thoughts.

You see, the Mind is like a projector; whatever you put into it, it will play that as your life experience.

But we did not need more thoughts at all. Instead, we needed less. So instead of identifying with the thought that we need more thoughts, we just need to recognize that thoughts are what need more thoughts; it was never us from the start. Remember thoughts are talking about themselves. We only believe them because they have an 'I' in front of them and

you guessed it, we believe we are this I. The Mind needs more knowledge because its nature as a void is to be without. However, our true nature is far from that; it is *All Knowing*.

You are not the thought 'I need to know more'; it never belonged to you.

The less you need to know, the more you will become aware of your infinite knowing.

I have to have everything go my way

We have been taught that to be truly successful and accomplished in life, we must have things go our way. We experienced sadness, hunger, or discomfort when we did not get our way and quickly discovered strategies to help us get our way.

We also learned that those who get their way have power and have a better life than those who do not. We saw Mom and Dad get their way over us, and that showed them up for having more power and having more in their lives than we did. We decided that it was important to get our way, because after all, our way is the best way.

The Truth is things cannot always go our way because often a better way exists. The more we need things to go our way, the more we decrease their chance at success and fulfilling their purpose. It is far better to be open to the best way than to assume our way is the best way.

In fact, you actually do not believe that your way is the best way. You doubt it, question it, and yet insist on it. Why? Because you believe it better to have a way than to be without a way. It is a substitute for knowing. It is uncomfortable to be without a way, so you insist on your way.

Instead, trust that there is knowing for the best way; it just has not revealed itself to you yet. But we still see our way as necessary to our survival the way we did as tiny children. We forgot that life has us in its warm embrace, and we decided that we need to look after ourselves. Instead of

having our way, there was another option to become aware of; a knowing, a gentle flow supporting us in life. There is knowing around everything.

It is not always clear to us, and it is okay to be without knowing. It does not make you dumb, stupid, or worse than others, because knowing does not exist in the Mind. Not knowing is an experience that comes from utilizing the Mind for answers. The other option is to simply be in stillness—that is the access to infinite knowing. It is better to go deep into emptiness rather than to supplement it with Mind-based thinking and force your way. You are not lesser for not knowing. You are greater for being aware of it.

But we do not feel safe in not knowing, which is why we must have our way. We do not feel safe in being disconnected from our knowing and worse, believing it does not actually exist. 'I do not have knowing' was a thought that got stuck in the Mind, but it was never ours.

'I do not know' is a thought, the void's thought, not our reality. The key take home here is, it's the Mind talking, telling you something you should pay close attention to.

Before thoughts, there was simply knowing. Having more thoughts does not take us closer to Knowing just further away. You do not need your own way, because it's the Mind's way of not knowing. The best way is knowing.

You are the knowing, not the void. Knowing is your way.

I am making bad choices

Do you ever feel that you are suffering in life right now because you keep making poor choices? Do you find yourself with too much clutter in the house, too much debt, and feeling poorly in your health because of the choices you make?

Forgive yourself. It is hard to feel good about ourselves and our choices when the Mind is full of opposing beliefs that leave us feeling empty, unfulfilled, needy, inadequate, damned if we do and damned if we do not.

We are making the right decisions and choices based on what we believe. In fact, you cannot make different ones until you believe differently. Are these choices bringing you happiness and contentment? Perhaps not. But neither are the beliefs you are still carrying around. We cannot expect a high quality of choices with poor quality beliefs.

The belief is that we expect ourselves to make poor choices and bad decisions. It is hard to do anything different when we believe this. But like all beliefs, this is just a thought that does not matter. It is just an idea we had about ourselves, and like countless others, it is no reflection of our Truth.

So, what is it a reflection of? The Mind—making poor choices and bad decisions. The Mind draws upon very limited knowledge, is often in a hurry, and is petrified of the consequences of both failing and succeeding. Of course, it will create stress in our lives; it is the source of all stress!

So, it is the belief that we expect ourselves to make poor choices, that makes poor choices, not us. We do not need to try and outsmart this, and the nervous energy it creates places a great deal of pressure upon us to get everything right.

What it points to is that the worst choice we ever made was swapping our true identity or Self for the thoughts in the Mind. This was a choice, a very poor one at that, that came from the belief that we have no choice. This led us to go with the loudest thing in our awareness—the Mind.

We learned to listen to what is loud—our parents' voices, police and ambulance sirens, screeching of brakes, and the words of our teachers and headmasters at school. Loud meant authority and time to listen. The Mind is loud, needs are loud, and these became the loudest thing in our lives.

You do not need to listen to what is loud, just what is true. The I is loud but not the Truth.

People expect the world from me

Do you ever feel that people do not get how truly amazing you really are? Do you feel frustrated if you do not receive validation from those around you for being all that you are?

This frustration is not actually coming from how others are seeing you, but rather that you chose to see yourself as the Mind. You've been looking for validation for this choice your whole life. That is what has us be more like others. The more we follow career paths, fashions, habits, interests, you name it, the more we all feel validated for all choosing to be the MIND.

The validation we really seek does not come from others it has to come from ourselves. The joke is we are asking our True-Self to validate our decision to not be our True-Self and praise us for spending an entire lifetime being the Mind. If this is not asking the "world" from our True-Self I don't know what is.

The irony is that people expect you to stay being the Mind so they feel validated for being the Mind. So, it is true to say people expect the world of you. In truth, it was never about you, just the Mind staying in existence. People can't expect this all they like, but the time for the Minds is running out.

"People expecting the world of me" is the thought talking about itself, whereas nothing is actually expected of you whatsoever.

The I's expect big things from themselves and each other, but we were never expected to believe we are the Mind.

I cannot allow myself to fail

Failure and the fear of failure can be quite debilitating for many, but unnecessarily so. The Mind wants you to think that failure is a real option. But often one of the scariest failures is that we will move away from something before it pays its dividends. This, to many of us, is the worst kind of failure: self-inflicted and abandoning on an idea, person, or project just before the payout.

It is better to realize that it is not the fear of missing out on the potential payout, but how much you will pay out on yourself. You are still terrified of making yourself horribly wrong for inaction, for not sticking with something or someone. You were told off so many times for quitting too early that you think all your failures in life stem from that.

The Truth is, there were many things you did not quit soon enough. Lots of your failures came from not quitting when you had the perfect opportunity. What causes you to stay too long is worrying that this might be the time you should stick it out. In most cases it is impossible for you to see that, except for a very small and subtle hint.

That hint is asking yourself if you are getting the outcome you intended for yourself. This determines how long you should stick with something. The fear is not wanting to feel stupid for quitting too soon, when you should have persevered. In reality, this fear stems from the fact that we have already quit something we should have persevered with. We quit on being ourselves before we even gave ourselves a chance.

When we are born, we are thrust into this world of I's. Everyone is an I. We chose to be an I before persisting at being without an I. This has stayed with us all these years, and it needs healing. We still feel raw for quitting on ourselves, and we fear we will keep doing it.

Back then we decided we were that which quits; we were the process of quitting itself. We identified with both. Realize that we are not the quitting we have believed we are. We are also not the quitter, as that was the thought: 'I quit at being myself.' It was this thought that quit, not us. We never actually quit at being ourselves; we just got swept away in identifying with the thought and believed that was who we are.

The I now fears we will quit at being an I. This is ok, but terrifying to the I. Instead of being an I, we can all choose to be a ME. ME stands for — My Everything.

I am not certain about anything

Do you find it hard to make decisions or choose between dozens of alternatives? Do you fear that no matter how hard you try, it is all a gamble, and you will most likely get it wrong anyway?

On the surface it feels like we believe we will get it wrong, so that is what we fear. But where I want to take you here is a different belief, that we cannot be sure of ourselves. If we cannot be sure of this, how can we possibly be sure of anything that comes out of us, such as making choices and deciding on things in life?

This originates from when as children we observed others seemingly so sure of who they were and what was what in the world. It baffled us that someone could be so sure of what they were made of when the jury was still very much out on understanding what we are and why we are here.

We were still in the evidence-gathering phase, piecing together who we were, what we were, what we were good at, and what we were not.

If people asked us a question we were unsure of, it put us into a spin. We believed we should know the answer; we should know what we want by now. Believing we should, is where the problem began. The belief that we should know ourselves was at play. Because of it and the pressure it created, we looked for ourselves and found ourselves in all the wrong places—in everything we were not!

From a space of being unsure, of being in the void, we looked to fill this void with answers. But the answers were empty, containing nothing more than beliefs around not really knowing what we are. If we were being certain about anything, we would have to say we are not. . . smart, liked, wanted, important. And so the Identity grew and grew.

Completing a sentence beginning with 'I am' is where the uncertainty started.

We knew that 'I am not' and 'I am' never felt right. So, what was unsure of itself was not us, but the 'I am'.

The snowball effect was that the I became very unsure of itself. How can something that is made up of beliefs ever be sure of itself? We too experienced being unsure of whether to see ourselves as this 'I am' character which added to our uncertainty in life. We chose to see ourselves as it, because what else were we do? Everybody else was, and who else would we be without it?

The best choice in that moment is to recognize that there is no need to become anything or anyone, nor a somebody, or not even a knowing of what or who I am. The need to know ourselves is something that has kept us trapped in the Mind's view of itself.

Realize: "Nothing that I am begins with 'I am' that we can be certain about! "

I cannot rely on myself or others

One of the hardest things in life for most of us is to trust that we will always have what we need to feel safe and secure. The problem comes from believing that we will never have all that we need to be safe and secure. We see it as an impossibility, no matter how much we have.

Underneath this, we believe that we will never be what we need, to have everything we need. This belief is tied to others like it, such as believing we will always screw everything up; we will get in the way of everything we need; we will never do what we need to do to have what we need; and we are not what it takes to have everything we need.

There is also another hidden belief that is the source of much stress, that we will never figure out what we need to do to feel secure and abundant. Much of this comes from the fear that we will never figure it out, but everyone else will, that we will be the only one who cannot figure this out.

The first Truth to realize is that there is nothing basic about figuring out how to support yourself financially during economic or personal hardships. To account for all variables, all economic or social climates, is nearly impossible. So, to give yourself a hard time about this is ridiculous.

Instead, you need to approach it with the knowing that you are enough; no matter what happens, you are enough. You are the one constant, and when you do not stop to see yourself as what it takes to be secure, that is where the insecurity is derived from.

The next Truth is that it was never about figuring anything out to be enough. No pathway or strategy will work because it would be coming from 'I am still not enough,' therefore creating that enduring experience of not enough in your life.

The confusion comes from the belief that your worth comes from what you have in the bank. But the Truth is that what you have in the bank comes from how much worth you see in yourself. This is because we began life learning to measure our worth from what is outside of ourselves—cars, houses, cash, reputation, and so on. Realize that trying to measure your worth in physical terms has no worth.

Realize that you are what it takes for all the inflow you need. All that is required of you, which you avoid, is the simplest thing: Hold a space for inflow. See yourself as the space for inflow. Seeing yourself as valuable on this Earth creates the wealth.

When the I says, 'I cannot rely on myself or others,' it is referring to all the beliefs and thoughts that make up the I. These are unreliable thoughts. The I cannot rely on itself, and we cannot rely on being this I either. It is doing us a favor by pointing this out.

Realize your value is beyond measure, so it is time to stop trying to measure your life now.

I do not know who I am

It is common to go through life living out what is expected of you, copying what others do, behaving as others behave, and making similar choices to those around you. We do this because very few of us ever had the answer to 'Who am I?'

Without this answer, we just did what was normal—study, get a job, get a mortgage, become discontent, have kids, struggle, get stressed, burn out, and so on. This pattern of doing the norm will continue until we are clear about who we really are. Of course, the belief that we do not know who we are prevents us from seeing any deeper and discovering the Truth. That is the problem with all the self-assessments we have taken over the course of our lives. By deciding and drawing a conclusion about ourselves, we block any further expansion or awakening within ourselves—or at least substantially slow it down.

This assessment of not knowing who we are stopped us in our tracks, and instead of getting us to realize a deeper Truth, we went with believing that we are our beliefs. The first mistake was to try and classify ourselves as any one thing. The second mistake was to box ourselves into needing to be a who, and the final mistake was believing we are an I that can or should assess itself.

In Truth, the self is best described as Being. Being is not confined to a body, let alone this one body. Being is the Universe experiencing itself across all forms—or better said, through every idea of itself. Therefore, no labels will do when being is everything, and ironically, being is nothing as well. It is ALL ideas. This is why we are happiest when we are simply being rather than trying to be any one thing. So the I was correct when it said, 'I do not know who I am.' The I is the collection of beliefs that is attempting to define itself in every moment. But you, the real you, does not have such a need. How else can expansion happen? If you keep imposing limits on how you see and define yourself, expansion is halted; if you allow there to be no limit to yourself, expansion keeps occurring. So, what we are really is an expansion upon all ideas of oneself, forever expanding.

Being allows us to keep expanding and seeing ourselves as more.

I am worried I am not doing a good enough job

When working or creating, do you experience a nagging voice in your head that constantly questions, whether you are doing a good enough job, or whether you are getting it right? This source of self-doubt can really take its toll on us, not to mention remove any joy we could be experiencing.

What causes this self-monitoring? On the surface it appears that we are striving toward a particular quality or standard and attempting to hold ourselves to that. We are trying to prevent failing in some form or another.

To fail would mean embarrassment, confrontation—or even worse, coming face-to-face with what we already believe, which is hiding underneath here. The belief at play is that we cannot get anything right on our own. This leads to a lot of fear and anxiety when we are trying to complete many different tasks or projects.

There are a lot of things going on here, including believing that people do not trust that we will do a good job, or will not like what we do in the end, or will move on from what we do. We believe we will not be celebrated, that others will do a much better job at this than we can. We believe we will not like what we do, that we are not special at anything, not worthwhile at doing things, even that we wish we were not doing this. Worse than all of these is this major belief that we are not allowed to be ourselves at doing anything.

How can we possibly feel equipped to complete anything when we do not believe we can do it our way or as ourselves? Let us face it, we will never feel confident doing something as anyone else but ourselves. This is where the massive anxiety comes from.

When we set out to do anything, we are often coming from the place of wondering how someone else would do it, how someone else would tackle it, see it, solve it, view it, understand it, finish it, sell it, or be seen because of it. We do not let ourselves be ourselves. That is because we believe that being ourselves will not do.

Of course, the Truth here is that being anyone else but ourselves will not do—and trying to please other people will not do either. We will forever feel as though we are failing if we focus on being someone else, achieving something their way, and so on.

We thought doing it someone else's way would be far more impressive than doing something our way. We believe that other people's way of doing things is better than our way and always has been. These beliefs are very painful. It is time to realize that other people's anything does not work for us and never will.

Realize that you are not here to look at yourself from somebody else's eyes; not meant to see how somebody else would see or do something. In fact, the I is somebody else; it was never you in the first place, so trying to be it will never do, and you will never feel 'enough' doing it.

This originates from having to choose which I we were going to be all those years ago. We worried that we will not do a good enough job making our selection. How can we? There is no I that comes close to the being we truly are, and no I that could ever do as good a job as us.

Simply choosing to even be an I, was us not doing a good enough job.

So, the problem arose when we identified with the thought that we did not do a good enough job. Identifying as this thought was never us, however. It is the thought itself that is not doing a good enough job.

Realizing that there is no need to be an I. In doing so is you doing the best possible job.

I have not done things the way I would have liked to

When we look back over our lives, many of us have accumulated countless regrets. Most of these are times when we have done something in a way and then wished that we would not have done it that way. We may have been pressured or felt obligated or coerced. Maybe we were trying to please a partner or simply being impulsive.

This experience of wishing we would not have done it this way will not go away by itself, and while we still have the beliefs behind this, we will keep reliving this same experience. The belief that creates this is introspective, that we are not the way we would have wanted ourselves to be. We believe that the pressures and events of life have made us into who we are today, but ultimately, we are not who we would rather be. Realizing that we have lived a lot of our life not really being ourselves becomes one of our biggest regrets.

This brings us to another belief of not being ourselves. When we are off kilter, we make decisions that are unlike us, and we create experiences we do not want. Being off kilter has resulted in many of the regrets that now haunt us.

What is behind this belief? On the surface, it is about the times we have been nasty to ourselves, the times we have been harsh and cruel, judging and punishing ourselves for experiences and decisions we have made. We know that being this way, was not us being ourselves.

And we are right—we were being something else—which brings me to the deeper aspect here. The belief that we are not ourselves is interesting, because it shows up that the I we have always related to as 'myself' is actually not myself. To be this I is not us being ourselves, and on some level we have always known this. The I would not have done many things in our life that we have done, and we would not have done many things the I has done.

But what we are most upset about doing is that we would not have called ourselves an I. We quietly think to ourselves that we would not have called ourselves all those horrible things that put us down, ridiculed us, abused us, belittled us, tortured us, flattened us—we would not have done that. But we did.

It was seeing ourselves as all these horrible things that caused us to make the decision to do these horrible things to ourselves in the first place. We must first realize that we are not what is horrible in life. The I, and all

those sentences that begin with I . . . have never truly reflected us, or the true idea that we really are.

There is a deeper you—a calm, loving, everything you—that does not need to regret having or being an I. It is now time to see yourself as something larger in life—as the love for yourself that you always were.

Realize: "Love is ME! There is no longer I … because I would not do it like that. There is no longer I am … because Love would not do it like that. Love is ME, because that is absolutely the way to do it."

If I am happy, someone will take it away from me

By the time many of us are adults, we have experienced countless disappointments in life. They take their toll physically and mentally, leaving many of us convinced life is out to get us or at least stop us in our tracks. It can become difficult to imagine a life without failures and disappointments. The good news is that these disappointments are about to be healed.

You are taught in life that you are the creator, the cause for what you experience, but one of the worst things to do is to believe that you are the cause of all the mishaps and tragedies you have experienced in life. Yes, you have played a role, but to blame yourself is a form of punishment, not empowerment.

The result of this self-blame game is a perpetual feeling of almost being cursed, that everything we do is no good and will inevitably result in some catastrophic failure or some all-consuming disappointment.

What is really at the heart of this? We worry that everything we do will result in failure and disappointment. But is there more to it? Yes! The belief underneath is that our lives will always be disappointing. And while that hits the spot, there is still something deeper, which is that we believe we are always a disappointment.

How can you create better than heartbreaking results with a belief like this in your space?

So, what is the real disappointment here?

We are disappointed that we believed we were a disappointment, and it was disappointing that we continued to live our lives believing ourselves to be a disappointment. This is very disappointing.

The deeper Truth is that there is nothing disappointing about being Love. What has been disappointing is carrying around a lifetime of beliefs that in no way reflect who we truly are. And we have been living the results of these beliefs and experiencing them in our life as if they are who we really are. Living the contents of your beliefs as your life is severely disappointing.

So, we were never disappointed in ourselves, but rather we were disappointed that we have substituted Truth-based experiences for belief, or identity-based experiences. That is hugely upsetting, especially when we know we could have experienced better.

We thought we were a disappointment because of how others reacted to us. In Truth we are disappointed in ourselves because we believed in others so much—in their thoughts, words, opinions, and assessments of us—that we took them on as fact. We were disappointed that we thought highly of very small people, and we thought lowly of ourselves for believing that we could ever be disappointing.

Realize: "As my Love-Self, I find there is nothing to be disappointed in.'

'Being my Love-Self creates more self-loving experiences, not disappointments."

I am going to make a huge mistake

Many of us fear making decisions, taking action, or starting something new because of the threat of making a huge mistake. But is it the mistake, or is it getting into trouble for our mistake that we fear most? It is less the mistake, but far more how we will feel about ourselves if we do happen to make a mistake.

Yes, we fear being told off by someone or losing something of value, like our money, home, car, or job, but what is worse is the fear of losing our self-image.

Our self-image is one of the most terrifying things we can ever lose—the very fragile view of ourselves that we work so hard to keep intact. Remember the way we felt when we got into trouble—all the horrible things we thought about ourselves? We worry about all the nasty things we will say to ourselves and how that will make us feel about ourselves in the event a mistake occurs. For example, we might have thoughts: 'I knew this would not work; I am a failure, after all. I always make stupid decisions. I hate myself; I always get it wrong.'

What is worse is what we extrapolate from all of this, that life will never get better; that we are stuck with an average self and an average life; or that we are stuck repeating the same patterns over and over again.

Realize that trying new, exciting things is not something to be angry at yourself for but something to congratulate yourself for. Imagine how upset you would be and what you would say to yourself if you spent your whole life never trying anything that inspired or excited you. That is really something to be upset about.

Our fragile self-image is false anyway. Trying to keep this intact is the incorrect path. So, rather than seeing your self-image as true and real, start seeing it as false. Be okay with changing how you end up seeing yourself. It can only get better from here. Making a mistake is not about upsetting your fragile self-image. The mistake is trying to protect it in the first place.

It is when we decided that we needed a self-image in the first place that we experienced ourselves making a big mistake. The belief that we need to see ourselves to collect ideas about ourselves was incorrect from the beginning. And the ideas we did collect about ourselves were also incorrect.

The trouble was that we believed we were the thing that was incorrect, instead of seeing the ideas we were collecting as incorrect. Choosing ideas was incorrect, and the ideas chosen were also incorrect.

You are not the idea that you need to have more ideas about yourself.

You are not what's incorrect, you are the observer of what has been incorrect.

I am wrong about everything in my life

When we are growing up and everyone in our life corrects us, it is easy to start believing that we are wrong about everything. But this damaging belief gets in the way of seeing the many times you have actually been right and all the times your way was the right way.

Some people went out of their way to make us feel wrong. This, of course, sent us into feeling that nothing we do will ever be right. In Truth it was them who were not being right by having us feel everything we do was wrong.

If we go a little deeper, one of the worst experiences for us was to agree with these people in our lives. When we sided with these naysayers and decided we were wrong about everything, it stuck, and a severe wounding occurred. It was bad enough that they were saying it, but for us to side with them was nothing short of devastating.

Interestingly, what was actually wrong was the idea that I could be wrong. The more we were criticized and corrected and made to feel bad, the more we believed that if our ideas, answers, actions, and beliefs are wrong, then there is something fundamentally wrong with us. The belief here is that everything we have decided about ourselves is wrong. Which ironically was correct, and still is to this day.

The notion that we must decide things about ourselves, and they must be correct and stand forever, is what got us into trouble in the first place. Defending these positions then made life difficult, and this became the source of all our reactions in life. The minute someone said anything that challenged what we decided about ourselves, an explosive reaction would occur—often more on the inside than on the outside.

So, it was not us that was wrong per se, just the need to make decisions about ourselves and defend what was not going to work for us—one of which is the need to be right about ourselves. This has created all kinds of havoc and kept many of these other beliefs firmly in place.

The result of this is that we attract suffering and hardship because we prefer being right about who we think we are. And we prefer being right to changing this belief and allowing in a much better life.

Even though it feels like we are getting everything wrong in life, and everything about us is therefore wrong, this was never about who we are at the core. It was always about who we decided we were that was never right in the first place. Furthermore, we never needed to be right about ourselves; in fact, it is so much more fun discovering that we are so much greater than what we decided all those years ago.

We were not right about ourselves back then, and we are not right about ourselves now, and we do not need to be! Trying to be right about ourselves leads to fighting with life, because life is saying that we are infinite, and we are arguing that we are not, that 'I am… this, that, and the other'. This never ends well.

Unimagine yourself. Be open, because the more open you are to being shown your greatness, the greater life can get. Instead of seeing yourself as everything about you being wrong, you can recognize that this is the I speaking about itself.

Everything about you is love, and therefore everything about you is lovable.

Having no idea about yourself is better than a Mind filled with incorrect ideas.

Realize: "Love is the best idea for me; it never ends, and it keeps on giving to all. It is easy to love that idea about me!"

I am not important and do not matter

So many of our beliefs have originated from this belief, and so many experiences of failure, rejection, and disappointment have resulted. It is easy to think that we are unimportant and do not matter because most of us were given very clear messages about this as children. We were taught that only adults are important. What do children know?

We were often not taken seriously, we were at the bottom ranks of the pecking order, and when we were truly in need or struggling, we may even have been told to shut up and grow up. We also learned that we came in last to money. We saw how much attention Mom and Dad gave to earning money and fighting over money, and how much respect they gave to wealthy people, and it became obvious that we were not what was important—that we did not matter.

Well, those were the conclusions we made, but what is really the Truth?

By now you might be able to see that the statement 'I am not important and do not matter' already has Truth in it. It is talking about the I here, not you. In that respect, it is correct, because the I is not real and has been made-up. What hurt us was the need to maintain this I—to be this I and hold onto it. Needing to be this I is what was not important and did not matter. We discovered that trying to be this I we believed we were, proved to be quite frustrating and full of disappointment. After all, it was never us in the first place.

But we can still feel the pain behind this, can we not? Why? Because we went to so much trouble deciding on what type of an I we were going to become. We conjured up this fictious character, one we sincerely believed would get us what we wanted in life. We thought it would fill us to the brim with joy, happiness, and love, and all it has done is create endless voids in our life. We are miffed that our idea of our I was so far off the mark.

Therefore, it hurts when we think that we are not important and do not matter. It is like starting a project, putting blood, sweat, and tears into it, only to discover it was all for nothing, and worse, it has caused more

problems than it solved. That is what we are dealing with now. Our I project was off the mark. But it was not in vain—and more importantly, it was important that we did that, and it mattered!

We created a lens through which to experience life, and it has been enriching. We believed we needed it at the time to avoid future struggles, and now we realize that time is up—the I project is no longer useful.

Having an I was important to explore everything you are not, and that matters on this planet.

The I that you came up with was important for my life experience; the one you chose mattered to you deeply. But having an I is no longer serving you, so it is no longer as important as you once believed, and it no longer matters as much as it once did.

Realize: "The I was talking about itself when it said 'I am not important and do not matter.' Never have truer words been spoken, so, it is time to let it go."

I am not appreciated

How often do we feel people around us just do not appreciate us? It is a common experience to be annoyed, frustrated, and even hurt that people do not recognize all our talents, skills, and abilities the way we would like them to. But is it other people we are annoyed at—or are we more annoyed at ourselves?

For most of our life, we have overlooked ourselves, thinking we need to be more like others. We have desired to be more knowledgeable, more skillful, and better looking because that is what we see in others. But what we have wanted even more is for us to be more knowledgeable, more skillful, and better able to see all our own talents, gifts, and abilities. We have been wanting to have the talents required to see what makes us so special.

The belief that we are without talent has led us to feel that everyone else is more than we are and has more to offer than we have. This all began by

being trapped in the thought that they can see their talents, but we cannot see our own. It was not that we wanted or were envious of their obvious talents per se; it is just that we were envious of their ability to recognize talent within themselves. That talent was very important to us, and we have wanted it ever since.

The perceived inability to see ourselves as talented is another hidden belief that causes much disappointment in ourselves. The Truth behind this is not that we were unable to see our own talent, but rather that we could not see or recognize other people's talents within ourselves. We made the mistake of looking inside of ourselves for the same talents others have. What we needed to see was that we are allowed to see different talents in ourselves than others, and we are allowed to recognize these talents in a different way to others.

The belief that we must have the same talents as others is yet another belief getting in the way of self-appreciation. Who can blame us for thinking this, when the school system was built to teach everyone to think the same, be able to do all the same things, in the same way, learning the same as one another? But even before that, we decided something deeper, that we must think the same thoughts as others. This is where the issue with self-appreciation really began, because in that moment we pushed ourselves off to the side and decided to be like everybody else.

And has our I not been true to that form? Therefore, we must keep pushing so much in life. Our I became so much like others that it became nothing like ourselves. It is difficult to change this because society keeps reinforcing how important it is to look at how great others are, rather than to look at how great we are. It is all over social media—everyone is always pointing out how great other people are. This became a refined talent for us to see talent in others over ourselves—so much so that we nurtured this talent over nurturing our talent to recognize talent in ourselves.

So, what is the Truth? We were not appreciating ourselves when we decided it is more important to appreciate others. We did not appreciate

leaving ourselves out in the cold. Nor did we appreciate not acknowledging all our talents when we were busy acknowledging everybody else's. What we forgot to realize was that our biggest talent is not needing to see others as better than we are. We are actually really talented at looking at ourselves.

The belief that we cannot see our own talents is about not being able to see our own talents while looking at everybody else's. In Truth, the I cannot see all our talents because it is made up of everyone else's. That is just the nature of the Mind.

Realize: "Seeing that 'I am not the Mind' is one of my biggest talents."

I need to be impressive

Many of us grow up learning that if we are not being impressive, we will not thrive in life. Our parents, teachers, and even friends would frequently point out other children that are excelling in every area of life. We learned who the genius was, who the best athletes were, who the wealthiest people were, who the most attractive people were. And of course, the media thrives on showcasing the most impressive people in the world. The industry is built upon that.

On a side note, no one ever pointed out to us who the happiest people in the world were—to me, they are the most impressive people.

It did not take much to put together that being impressive equals more attention, more money, a better life, and a happier you. It became so ingrained in us that the need to be impressive carries into virtually every activity in our life. How we dress, how we style our hair, what brand of clothes we buy, what we watch on television, what we study, what careers we choose, what partners we are attracted to, how much money we need to earn, what we say or do not say in public, how well we age, how much cosmetic surgery we should have—the list never ends!

The need to be impressive haunts us all the time, and it does not stop when we finally ARE impressive, because achieving what the need says we need, does not heal the need. I have mentioned several times, that to do

what the Mind says to do and achieve all the outcomes the Mind says will make all the difference, does not actually make any difference. Following the need will not resolve the need.

In fact, having the need to be impressive not only keeps you constantly striving to be impressive, but also robs you from ever experiencing the satisfaction that is meant to come from being impressive when you achieve that. It is a double whammy! The result is that you cannot even feel or celebrate all those times you have been impressive, despite all the hard work and dedication you put in to being impressive.

So, what is the Truth? We wanted to be impressive because it was the nearest sensation to feeling love. We believed that if we are impressive, then we can love ourselves. But what was impressive was not the act of being impressive to others, but the idea that we deserve love, and we want to give it to ourselves. That is a very lovable idea—and impressive!

What was not so impressive was the idea that we need to impress others to receive love, that got tangled inside of this mess. It in turn led to beliefs like needing others; thinking what they think matters; believing how they see us matters; and so on.

The Truth hiding here is that it is impressive that we want to love ourselves. We—or better said, love—gets to see how amazing we are and how worth loving we are. But we never needed to be impressive to see that; we only need to see that we are worth loving and that is enough.

"Love is worth loving, and the real me is all that love doing and being the love that is worth loving. We are Love Being; love is my beingness."

I am a mistake

Do you ever feel as though your whole life has been a mistake? Did you grow up believing your parents regretted ever having you? Many of us took on the belief that we are a mistake, and this has caused everything from depression, decision anxiety, and even illness. It is one of the most debilitating beliefs to have and can often be one of the trickiest to clear. It makes

us think that everything we do is a mistake. It makes us feel unwanted and unloved, and it makes us believe that there is no possible future where we will not make some huge mistake.

Despite what our parents thought about us or did not think about us, this comes down to how we saw ourselves as children. We were the ones assessing ourselves and our place, and then deciding what view of ourselves would work best. And this is where the huge mistake happened. Instead of recognizing the way the world works as a mistake, we took on the view that we are the mistake. The good news is that we were never the mistake. How could such a sublime life form ever be a mistake on this Earth? Life is never a mistake.

We took on the identity of being a mistake, rather than seeing that the real mistake was to ever take on an identity in the first place. We witnessed everyone around us collecting new traits to identify with. It was the done thing, and still is. We innately knew we were so much more, but we caved and compromised into belonging. The way we did this was to take on the views others held about themselves and adopt them for ourselves. And in that moment, we decided that this process of 'I am' was a huge mistake!

We quickly realized that to label ourselves with the prefix 'I am' was the biggest mistake we could ever have made, and it was going to be a severe prison sentence for life. To say 'I am' limits us to being the energy of that sentence. We were never meant to take on that 'I am. . .' anything specific. And instead of seeing it as a mistake, we decided that we are that mistake—it just occurred.

Then we kept adding to our collection of 'I am this'; 'I am that', which led us further and further away from our innate Truth. The originating mistake was deciding that we are the mistake of labeling ourselves as an 'I am'. We identified with the mistake, seeing ourselves as the mistake of that decision.

But we were not the mistake being made—we were the ones watching a mistake occur. It can be said that we are what came before the mistake to

call ourselves 'I am'. Better said, there was love—ME—and then a decision to identify with the idea of 'I am', and then the realization that was a huge mistake to identify as anything. Then we called ourselves a mistake.

The Truth is that we did not know better than to fit in. Everyone was doing the 'I am' thing, so we took that on and very quickly realized it was not a smart move, and we have been calling ourselves that mistake ever since.

The best thing we could have done was to acknowledge to ourselves that we do not need a self—not one that identifies with opinions and judgments. As such not needing to be an 'I anything'. An infinite being is a far more apt description of what we are, or a Being being infinite. Therefore, to be any kind of 'I am' fails to capture our true nature.

There is a tendency in the spiritual community to identify simply as 'I am' as a way of seeing oneself as God energy. If this works for you, great. However, the word I for most of us summons the I identity, so you may prefer the pronouns 'ME', 'the All', or simply 'my Love-Self'.

The realization is that we are not the identification process, and we did not make the mistake of identifying with limited and small ideas of ourselves. Furthermore, we did not invent that process, so why identify with it at all? It was never our idea of ourselves; we came with infinite ideas of ourselves, not the 'I am' idea. It was never us in the first place! What is more is that identifying with being the mistake of identifying with 'I am' was not even the mistake. The only mistake was to think that we could never again let those small ideas go and become anything different. That was never our Truth.

As a Universal Being, as Love, as the All, it is our choice to experience ourselves as everything all at once, or as single things one at a time.

We were never stuck being any one thing, because our Truth is as a being that is all things."

Realize: " The ALL is ME; the 'I am' is the void."

I need to be liked

We have touched on many needs, such as the need to be impressive and the need to receive attention, but one stands out above the rest: the need to be liked. It shows up as us wanting to avoid failures, embarrassments, confrontations, and rejections; and desiring success, wanting to look good, hoping we are getting things right, being impressive, and standing out from the crowd.

The question is: Was it ever us that we wanted to be liked? It feels like all we have ever wanted is to be liked, but when we look much deeper—and by now we are all ready to do so—what we wanted to be liked was not actually us, but what we came to believe about ourselves. The more beliefs we adopted, the more insecure we became with our new self—the Mind self.

We had a suspicion that what we were taking on board was questionable, so validation and outside opinions became a necessity. The more we doubted our interpretation of ourselves, the more outside validation we needed.

The heart of this doubt was the idea that we do not like ourselves, meaning that we disliked what we had now come to believe is ourselves. And because we did not like it, we were hoping maybe others would. Thus began the intense need to be liked.

In Truth, we did not need to like the beliefs we took on as ourselves, and we certainly did not need others to like the beliefs and identity we took on as ourselves. But we thought that was the game, as we saw everyone else around us trying to get others to like the idea of themselves that they had concocted for themselves. The real us did not require being liked; it just required questioning the taking on of beliefs about ourselves that we do not even like.

Why did we do that? We did it to see how they would fit, what they might create, and ultimately because we thought we would be right in doing so. But the beliefs were not an accurate portrayal of our true nature,

which is why we did not like them. The beliefs wanted to be liked; the Mind wanted to be liked for all that it was becoming, but we were not budging.

We could see that the beliefs were not likable, so we disliked this version of ourselves. It stuck ever since, until we forgot that it was never us, but just ideas of us. That is when the next non-likable act happened. We disliked ourselves for holding onto this non-likable version of ourselves. We asked ourselves subconsciously why we are believing in this, and the longer we kept asking, the less we liked ourselves for it. We even began to distrust ourselves and started to believe that we cannot be trusted, which gave rise to a whole bunch of new beliefs and issues to contend with.

In the end, all we had to see was that the I that we invented cannot be trusted, because it was never us in the first place. And not liking beliefs was our way of navigating away from them because they, too, were never us in the first place.

The ultimate realization here is that whatever is unlikable was never the true us in the first place, so we can safely let go of what we never liked about ourselves.

"What I could have called myself, what I could have associated as my I, is the spark of consciousness that was witnessing this new reality taking shape, that was always ME—a genius, a white light, capable of seeing all the Truth in the world and encompassing that as the fullness of what is me."

Going back to the Spark is what this book is all about!

I am not allowed to have any fun in my life

Have you reached the place in life where you feel either because of your job, your expenses, your spouse, or your children that you are simply not allowed to have fun in your life? Do you secretly wish you were much younger again, back to a time you were carefree, without responsibilities, obligations, and no longer feeling tied to anyone or anything?

There is a very damaging belief at play here that has us feel that all the good times are over! It has us believe that life cannot possibly be joyful again, and it has us point the finger at someone in our life because it is all their fault! So, what is the belief? It is that we cannot allow ourselves any more joy; it is time to take life seriously.

So despite wanting to blame various people in our lives for experiencing little or no joy, you guessed it, we are the ones responsible. We refuse to let joy in. We block it, squash it, avoid it, even fear it. Why? There are several reasons for it. We came to believe that joy is no longer good for us; joy gets us into trouble; the need for joy is holding us back in life; our experiencing joy causes pain to others; and even that joy makes us weak.

Much of these associations came from being yelled at as children for having too much fun and being told to grow up, take life more seriously, or worse, being told that our joy comes at the expense of other people. We soon decided that joy must be had in very small doses, if at all.

Eventually this embargo we placed on joy led to us resenting ourselves, and that is where many of us find ourselves now—full of anger, resentment, and an inability to experience more joy in our lives.

So, what is the Truth?

There is a hidden belief that we are not allowed to enjoy being ourselves. This led to us shutting joy out of our lives. What happened was that we experienced the thought that it is not safe or okay to be ourselves, and once we decided that it became obvious that it is no fun being ourselves, so we decided that as well.

As soon as we decided that it is not okay being ourselves, all the fun, joy, and playfulness went out the window. We were upset at ourselves for ever believing that it is not okay to be ourselves, and we still are upset at ourselves for believing it.

What we meant was that it is not okay to take on all these beliefs about ourselves, and that it is not okay to believe in them as if they are ourselves.

We also felt that it is not okay to take on what others are saying about us as beliefs to then experience as ourselves. It was this listening to what others say about us that was not fun. By doing this, we got to see that being us is no fun and hurts. We decided that taking on beliefs about ourselves is no fun.

In Truth, however, it was not us that was no fun; it was experiencing the beliefs as ourselves that was no fun. And that is the trouble with beliefs. They may seem like a bunch of words, but they are a prescription for a very specific experience. It is like computer code. If you take on the code, you will experience the full intention behind that programming. And we have been taking on these lines of code left, right, and center, prescribing for ourselves very specific experiences and outcomes.

We are not the process of taking on beliefs, and most importantly, we are not the idea that "I should even be taking on new beliefs", because taking on new beliefs is dangerous.

We are not what is left over after taking on all these damaging beliefs. That upset, that pain, that anger, and that hurt were never me. That is exactly what is not me!

If I do not force myself, I will not get anywhere in life

Ever since an early age, our parents led by example and taught us that without force, life will not work to our advantage. We are forced to eat food we do not want, sleep when we are not tired, take car trips we do not want, meet people we do not like, and attend school no matter what. We were told there would be consequences if we did not do what was asked.

If you did not eat your dinner, there would not be any TV. If you did not do your homework, you would never amount to anything. We came to believe that we must force ourselves to do something to get to a better, more important place in life than where we are at now. And a lot of us are in a better place financially because of this.

But what are the consequences of forcing our mental and physical well-being? Is force really the strategy meant for us? The answer is no. To force yourself is to take yourself away from what comes most naturally. In society, we make our natural flow wrong. We believe that if we are not striving or being ambitious, we will end up with nothing.

So, what is the Truth? There is no better place than right here; forcing anything upon ourselves takes us out of the peace that right now is offering us. Peace creates sanity, sanity creates health, and both make for a much better life. Force is only needed because we do not trust that we will get there by being ourselves.

It is force that causes us to resent, rebel, and refuse. It is not the fear that we will not get anywhere that scares us; it is the fear of what we will do to ourselves to make us get somewhere that scares us.

You may have guessed what is at the very heart of this. It is the experience very early on of forcing different ideas and labels on ourselves. One of the biggest uses of force was the idea that we must force ideas on ourselves. We believed that we must make ourselves believe what we are telling ourselves, and we must make ourselves believe what others are telling us.

Going deeper, we also forced ourselves into believing that we must have beliefs to get anywhere in life. That was very clearly the Mind talking, because without be**lie**fs—the Mind, the void—would not grow. The opposite was our Truth.

Without beliefs you will experience yourself as all things, as everywhere, right now.

I cannot finish what I start

Many of us begin projects with excitement and determination, but partway through something, we reach a blockage. We experience dread at the idea of continuing, this dread turns to stress, anxiety, and overwhelm, and before we know it, this is yet another project that never comes to fruition.

What is happening here? Is it that we were never meant to finish the project? Or are we holding ourselves back in some way? First, let us not see any project as a necessity; let us see that each project experience is a mirror. Often what occurs is that we realize we will be exposed, warts and all, to others if we complete something. We fear that others will see that our quality of work is not all we hoped it would be, so we fear being seen as a disappointment.

What is worse, we fear that we will see that our quality of work is not the high standard it should be—meaning we are at not the high standard we have been convincing ourselves we are at. The ugly truth is that we already believe our quality of work is not good enough—that we are not good enough. We attempt projects in the first place to help overcome feeling that who we are and what we do is never good enough.

The Truth is that the disappointment came a long time ago from needing to feel good about what we do. We stopped doing things for fun and did them to feel good about ourselves and who we are. The disappointment starts when the project starts, not when it ends. It starts with the decision that we need to do this to show ourselves that we are better than we think we are.

Right there we start by being in a state of disappointment, and how we start is how we will end. The Truth is that we do not need projects to show us how great we are, because we never needed to prove to ourselves how great we are.

Let us go a little deeper, because there is more to realize. Hidden underneath this need to feel good about ourselves and this need to see more from ourselves is an idea that never actually got finished: We cannot finish a thought about ourselves.

This is interesting because on the one hand, it has left us petrified that to finish a thought about ourselves could end up being horrible, and on the other hand, we were entirely correct—we should never finish a thought or

idea about ourselves because it is doomed to be incorrect no matter how special or expansive that thought or idea intrinsically is.

We came to realize that we must never finish a thought about ourselves, so we left all our thoughts half-created. By half-created, I mean we used the term 'I am'. As soon as we did this, it became half about us and half about the 'I am' character. The description was intended for us, but deep down we knew we were not the 'I am' in this sentence.

Inadvertently we have left ourselves with a plethora of unfinished thoughts, ideas, and realizations about ourselves. The true realization is that we are not to have any thoughts about ourselves because the 'I am' is not us having any thoughts about ourselves. Furthermore, the 'I am' needs to feel good about itself because it keeps having horrible thoughts about itself.

Realize: "It is not my job to finish these thoughts, or improve upon them, as it was never me having them in the first place. Therefore, these thoughts were also never me, and never about me, so why would I need to correct them? Why BE the need to correct them? That was never me either."

You are not the need to correct these thoughts, finish them, or improve them, it was the I who seeks better thoughts about itself—but it was never you, as having thoughts about yourself was never necessary.

I need to compete with others to succeed

We live in a very competitive world. Every day we see people, families, schools, places, countries, companies, celebrities, and sports teams compete against one another. We see creatures in nature compete for survival all the time.

Competition is very much accepted as the norm on this planet, and so we believe that competition is a healthy way to be, that it brings out the best in us. There are many problems with this idea, one of which is that

competing makes us feel that we must be the same as others, just better. This is where many of us get off-track.

It is a mistake to believe we are all meant to be the same. We think we are meant to think the same, act the same, know the same, learn the same, and achieve the same. The irony is that every one of us came to this Earth to be different from one another.

Competing does not cause us to succeed; it is being different that lets us thrive. Everyone being the same is hurting all life on Earth, and so there is great effort by the Universe to shake up the norm and alter the convention. We are not meant to succeed at being the same by succeeding like others, but rather, we are meant to succeed at not being the same. That is the success we long for.

Where this began, of course, was at the thought level, when we watched others try to have the same thoughts about themselves that we wanted for ourselves. We believed we must think a certain thing about ourselves to like and appreciate ourselves. We believed if we cannot hold onto this thought about ourselves, we will fail dismally and end up unhappy.

We watched others want the same thoughts, and we began to compete for them, believing we needed to be these thoughts. This had us push in certain directions to strive to be great at certain things so we could be the thoughts we were desperate to hold onto and claim as our own. Some of these thoughts we wanted to be and own were: 'I am a winner'; 'Everyone loves me more'; 'I am more interesting'; 'I am more respected and admired'—you get the gist.

In Truth, it is not that we even needed the experience of succeeding; we just wanted to feel justified in hanging onto these thoughts about ourselves, such as 'I am more successful'. Having the thought and keeping the thought was the trophy. 'I am that thought' is what we wanted to say about ourselves—'I knew I was that thought'. Every time we failed to be that thought, to accurately represent that thought, we would experience intense failure.

The need to compete to have a thought is interesting, because there is no shortage of thoughts; there is no regulatory body controlling ownership and no license to being or claiming a thought as your own. So why the need to compete for them? Well, this came from the need to replace the Truth about ourselves with non-truth.

Non-truth began competing against what was true and real about ourselves. We ended up in competition with what we knew was true versus what we wanted to claim as true. For example, we knew we were limitless, but many of us wanted to believe that we are more important than others. In a space of being limitless, there is no need to be more important, and more importantly there is no need to be something so limiting as a thought. The need to be a thought was competing with an absence of a need to be any one thing—truth versus non-truth.

Our Truth is that we do not have to be labeled anything. We do not need a thought about ourselves. What is more is that those thoughts wanted to be our identity, squeezing their way into the Mind to take over. Sounds crazy, right? Well, this book is not called *Losing Your Mind* for nothing!

Thoughts are still competing to be us; that is the void wanting to be seen as us. So, what is the Truth?

You are not the thought 'I have to be a thought,' and you are not the need to have an idea about yourself. You never needed to claim an idea about yourself; it was always better to have no-idea about yourself—that is the way of the limitless self.

I need to be sad over my past

We often see life being portrayed in television and movies as very glamourous as we see people rise to fame and success. We have been told to aim high, think big, and achieve anything we set our Minds to. We heard our parents share success stories and times of happiness, pointing to others who have achieved incredible lives.

So where does this leave us? For many, it inspires greater ambition, the need to strive and push even harder toward successful outcomes. But the double-edged sword of striving is the feeling of regret and sadness for the times we fell short of living a great life.

It is very easy to think back over stressful times, regrettable decisions, and times when we executed poor judgment. The problem with living in the past is that it consumes our present and can easily become our future.

How do we avoid doing this when we know it's unhealthy for us? First of all, we must recognize a belief at play here, that if we pity ourselves for our past, we do not need to feel as much of a failure as we otherwise would. We get something from feeling sorry for ourselves; that is why we do it. But what we think we are getting is of no value whatsoever.

We believe that if we feel sorry for ourselves, it helps to not label ourselves a failure. But that is exactly what we are doing—labeling ourselves as a failure, which is what is giving rise to our self-pity. We are trying to like ourselves just a little bit more than we otherwise could, hoping that self-pity would do the job.

The belief is that if we label ourselves, others will like us. We are trying to be likable to others, and we give ourselves whatever label we think will do the job. This began years ago as we were deciding what label to take on so others would accept us, embrace us, be kind to us, and love us.

We chose some doozies, including 'I am sad'; 'I am alone'; 'I need attention'; as well as some better ones like 'I am always happier than others'; 'I solve things for people'; and 'I make people feel good about themselves'. We, of course, decided that we were these beliefs, and we identified with them.

We also identified with the need to even choose a label to get through life more successfully. This was a need, and we also chose to see ourselves as this need and as the beliefs that would quench this need. But we were

never the need to get by in life. We were never the need to make life more successful for ourselves. We were never needy.

In Truth we never needed a better outcome in life. Why? Because entering life on Earth was already the best possible outcome. There could be no greater outcome than that, no matter what was experienced or achieved post being born. Sounds odd, does it not? That is because we undervalue the birthing process, and we fail to see that simply being alive is the achievement we were always hoping for.

The important realization is that we never needed more to have a great life experience. We never needed a better experience in life, nor any labels to get by, just to see that we are alive. Trying to succeed never mattered—but being born did in every way!

The I is sad that it missed this huge, momentous event because it was concerned with becoming more ideas about itself. It is still sad about this today. Adding new ideas is not the experience we think it is; letting old ideas go is the experience we have been searching for.

We never needed more labels or to have more of anything to be great.

I can't create success

Success means different things to different people. But something we all can agree on is that it is meant to offer an experience of joy and contentment. We work hard to create success, but often two things happen. One, we do everything in our power to sabotage success from entering our lives; and two, we are unable to see success when we finally allow it in, and it is staring us in the face.

This is because on a deeper level we are really saying to ourselves that we must not allow ourselves to see what makes us great. Why would we do this? Because we also believe that we make others suffer. We decided this as young children, and we have never recovered from believing this, nor forgiven ourselves, for that matter.

To believe we are the cause of other's unhappiness and dissatisfaction in life makes it nearly impossible to see our own greatness, because instead of celebrating ourselves, we are stuck in punishing ourselves. As children, we were made to feel bad so others around us did not have to blame themselves for ruining their own lives.

But what was happening on a deeper level will really amaze you. As we began to claim new ideas as our own, new beliefs to represent us, we quickly discovered that these ideas affected or bumped into other people's ideas that they chose for themselves.

So, we decided that our ideas are the cause of other people's unhappiness. What we did not realize was that the only reason people were getting annoyed at us for this, is that they chose even worse ideas for themselves than we chose to represent us. This became a mirror for them as they confronted those around them with all their poor choices. It was not our choices or ideas that made people unhappy; it was their own ideas they chose for themselves that made them unhappy.

It does go a bit deeper, so let us explore. We came to realize something confronting for ourselves, and that's that if the ideas we have chosen to represent upset others, what if they are also upsetting us? This began our discontent with the basis of the identity we had chosen for ourselves. It also began the belief that we are discontent with what we chose to be ourselves. As usual, we also became that disappointment as well, believing that we are the disappointing choices we made for ourselves.

So what is the Truth, even if it might sound like a Dr. Seuss book, is that we were never the need to make others feel better about themselves; it was their job to make better choices for themselves about themselves; we were never the need to make better choices for ourselves, about ourselves, and we were never the ideas we chose to represent ourselves; we were not the disappointment we experienced based on the poor choice of ideas we made about ourselves. That was never us. We thought we let others down with our poor choices, but we let ourselves down. We were hoping to make

successful choices for ideas to represent us; we were hoping to be the success behind making successful choices.

What we can claim as successful was, in fact, our attempt to improve our lives by making choices in the first place. We were trying to better our lives; we just did not realize that not choosing any ideas was the best choice. Furthermore, we believed that success is not us; we are not success, because there was a knowing within us that to make any choice is not a successful outcome.

So, we robbed ourselves of identifying with success because we scorned ourselves for choosing ideas and thoughts to identify with in the first place. The second we had the thought that we must be a thought; we must choose a thought to be successful, we knew we had dropped our bundle on ever seeing ourselves as successful.

By the way, if you are starting to understand how important it is to help children have the right thoughts growing up, then kudos to you! Staying away from identifying with thoughts, ideas, and beliefs that can in no way ever represent their enormity, is the most important education a child can have.

Realize: "We are not the need to be a thought; it is the I—the Mind—that needs that."

You are not the need to be successful. You never needed to avoid identifying as thoughts to be successful; You just needed to see that needing more thoughts does not make you successful.

If I complete something, I will fail

We have hopes and dreams that someday we will achieve big things in our life. But often when that day gets closer, something happens inside of us to put on the brakes. It may be experienced as stress, fear, panic, or even illness. But it is actually the fear that someday we may fail in such a big way that our whole Identity will be called into question. Which, ironically, is what we are all here to do.

Despite this, the fear is too great. It is an act of self-sabotage. Inside, self-protection has been activated to stop us from ruining our lives. This protection is the sabotage. What are we protecting ourselves from? We fear that soon people will see us for the frauds we believe we are. And what is worse, we think we are about to come face-to-face with the realization that we never did know anything, and we were never ever good at anything.

These are huge fears coming straight out of our childhood. The reason they feel so palpable is that they are not in our future; they are here and now in our present and throughout our past. We have been carrying them around nearly our whole life. We think we are preparing and protecting ourselves from imminent failure, but deep down we believe we already are the failure.

The failure, of course, goes much deeper than what we can usually remember. It began when we decided we must let go of our infinite nature to get somewhere in this lifetime. The thought was along the lines of needing to label to define ourselves. The idea was that to discover ourselves, we must define and establish our boundaries, who we are, where our limits are, and so on. We, of course, could not see or feel any, so we believed the best way to do that was to label ourselves, thereby instigating a parameter around our nature.

But instead of this helping us to discover our true expansiveness, we inadvertently caged ourselves into the labels we decided upon. Well, we got the labels wrong—at least, that is what we believed—and we felt as though we had failed dismally at our attempt to capture a snapshot of ourselves.

The failure was not in our approach, but in having the idea that we need to define ourselves. We insisted on this, and the more we did it to belong in the world, the more we began to feel like an even bigger failure. Any attempt to define ourselves is inaccurate, so how can we feel like a true success if we think true success comes from labeling ourselves—even if the label is a true success?

The idea that we need to label ourselves as a success to be a success is what caused all the problems. And how many of us have been trying to label ourselves a success by doing what we think successful people do? Once we give ourselves a label, we cannot help but justify keeping this label by doing what is required to maintain it. But it was needing to have the label in the first place that caused us to feel unsuccessful from the start.

Thinking that we need certain labels, or to strive for certain labels, and then to maintain certain labels in order to be successful, to feel successful, and see ourselves as successful, are all incorrect ideas.

The Truth was far simpler than that, as it always is. The need to be successful was never our need; it was part of the void, the I. The need for successful labels was never our need; it was also part of the void. The failure we felt was letting go of being without needs and instead believing that the Mind's needs are our needs.

You never needed to add to your needs to feel as successful as others, who believed having more needs meant becoming more successful. The less needs you have, the clearer you see yourself.

I am not allowed to receive

Many of us growing up were taught to behave by our parents taking things away from us, or at least threatening to do so. We also watched how they took things away from themselves, refusing to allow joy into their own lives, punishing themselves and putting themselves last for others. This is something they learned from their parents growing up.

It did not take long for us to decide a cluster of very negative beliefs, such as it being wrong for us to receive, not being allowed to receive, not deserving to receive, being destined to never receive in my life, that everyone is entitled to receive but not us, that we will always be left out, that it is normal to switch off joy in our lives and that if we do not receive, others cannot hurt us. With these beliefs in the way, it becomes very difficult to let in the fullness of life.

We learned not to receive because of other people in our lives—either out of fear and the need to protect ourselves, or out of spite to gain some semblance of power over their threats. The effect on us has been devastating. To deny receiving is to deny living. How do we mend this?

We mend this by realizing that we do not need to hurt ourselves to show others that we are not okay. We do this to get attention, but the attention we need is because we are sad from not allowing in enough of what we need. The next realization is that we can let in the fullness of life, because in our relationship with life, there is just us and life; no one else can get in the way of us receiving what we need. We can have what life wants to give us, and we want that now.

It is important to go deeper to see that this originated from a very early thought that we are not allowed to have more of what we want. But this was pointing to the idea that we are not allowed to have more thoughts about ourselves, and that we are not allowed to conclude more things about ourselves. We were attempting to conclude that we were loved, happy, and have what we need, but we were denied the ability to conclude those things about ourselves. In the realm of thoughts, they were being withheld from us.

Why? We believed these thoughts were beyond us, out of our reach, and must be earned somehow. We believed that we cannot have those thoughts, and we have felt that we must earn happiness ever since. The idea that we are happy is a thought, a conclusion about oneself; it is not an object or something physical you can acquire. But we still believe that thought is out of our reach. Ironically, we thought happiness came from acquiring the thought 'I am happy; I can be happy with myself.'

Essentially, we believed that we need the thought 'I am happy' to be happy. But in that moment a need was created—the need to have the thought 'I am happy,' and from that moment on, we could not be happy without having that thought. It set up the need for us to have things to be happy. What is worse, we identified with the thought 'I need to be happy',

thereby becoming the full expression of that thought. We added another need to the pile.

As we are intrinsically not the same substance as a thought, we battled with the dissatisfaction resulting from never being able to be the thought 'I am happy'. It is not what we are, but we are not less than that thought, and that is where the confusion came from. Instead of seeing ourselves as everything else the Universe is, we got stuck on wanting to be this thought and wanting to be the need to be this thought.

Ultimately, we were settling for seeing ourselves as something smaller than what we really are. This caused the initial unhappiness and has resulted in repeating unhappiness in our lives, as we are still trying it on. We often think we are unhappy because we do not get to see ourselves as bigger, better, richer, or more important, but it is the need to still see ourselves as these smaller ideas that makes us truly unhappy.

So, if we are bigger than the thoughts 'I am happy' and 'I need to be the thought I am happy', what are we really? We have no-need to be less than what we are. We were never the thoughts themselves—far from it. In other words:

We are the infinite that supports all ideas, all thoughts to exist and experience themselves grow and evolve and be experienced by someone or something. But we are not the substance called 'thoughts' and we can never be them, only feel them.

I need approval from others

Do you ever feel that your ideas, your creations, are not quite finished until you hear what others think of them? Do you experience needing to know what others think to help form or cement your own view of what you have created or come up with?

Many of us have been taught to care more about what everyone around us thinks about us than what we think of ourselves. For some, this has

become so ingrained that we believe what we think is irrelevant, and what matters is what others think.

This is because of the beliefs that "our opinion does not count, other people know better than we do, and other people's opinions are better and hold more weight than our own." These beliefs are really all about the same thing, but they can trip us up in different ways.

As a result, we find it very difficult or impossible to ever believe in ourselves, to ever see that what we think, what we create, or what we say is ever good enough. It leaves us constantly second-guessing ourselves, never truly able to form a solid and positive opinion about anything we do.

How can we ever truly move forward and enjoy our lives if we are forever questioning whether what we do, say or create is good enough?

This originated from being unsure of the new thoughts we were deciding on in our early years. We were forming new ideas about ourselves based on the ideas other people were feeding us. We heard others speak to us in a particular tone, say certain things to us, and even say certain things to themselves, and this fed what we took on for ourselves.

But even the idea to take on new thoughts and ideas was questionable. So, we began looking at others to see how they went about taking on new ideas, and we saw them taking on plenty. What puzzled us was how little everyone scrutinized the ideas they were taking on and throwing our way. It occurred to us that as they were older, wiser, and more assertive than we were, they must know what they were doing, so we should do the same.

In that moment we decided that others know more about this than we do, others can see more than we can, and if we do not listen to them, we might make a mistake and screw up. We decided that others are the authority, clearly know more than we do, and are better judges of what should work, more than we could ever be.

Suffice to say, this was completely incorrect.

We identified with the thoughts: 'Others know more than I do'; 'I should look to others to know what I do not know'; 'I should seek others' opinions of what my I should look like'; and 'If others approve of my ideas, then I must be on the right track.' We were using others to help us form our I.

The result is that to this very day, we are relying on others to reinforce that the I we chose all those years ago is still the correct one. When we do not get validation and approval, we end up in a downward spiral. The reason is that we have been questioning our I for years, always seeking whether we made the right choices in what we included in this Identity.

The moment we do not get validation, we come face-to-face with the thought that we knew we were choosing the wrong thoughts for our I. This is very upsetting, as we have spent our whole life trying to hold up this flimsy I.

We came to believe that our I needs approval, because we did not like what we have included in it. We did not like the I we made up, because it literally came from everyone else. It makes sense that we did not like it, and it makes sense that only others could like it, and because we did not like it, we looked to others to like it.

This I was not about us; it was just a collection of ideas other people took on as themselves. It was not a reflection of us in any way, shape, or form. There was no chance of us ever being sure of this self, as it was a false representation of our True Self. To live with a false self, made up from others, means that we will always need approval from others.

"I need approval from others" is just a thought—a thought about the thought itself needing approval from other thoughts. It never represented our True Self, which has no such need.

I need more money

Earlier we explored the belief 'I need money'. We got to see that it is the I that has the need for money, not us. The trouble is that this need feels so real, it is such an intrinsic part our reality, that it can be very difficult to become free from it.

The irony is that we believe the more we have this need, the more money we will make. The opposite is the Truth, as is always the case with the Mind. The Truth is that as we evolve beyond this need for more money, as we let go of having this need, the easier it becomes to make greater sums of money.

So where is this need really coming from? For many of us, growing up we saw that money meant power. We watched our parents have all the decision-making power over whether we got what we wanted—a treat, a toy, an experience, or even pocket money. We quickly decided that we need power, which was another way of saying we need money. But it was not money we were really longing for; it was freedom from how we were feeling without power.

We felt powerless over making decisions. They were just happening around us and for us, without us being able to exert any real influence. It was frustrating. So we decided, that we have no power over what happens around us or to us. So, what did we do to help us move away from this feeling? We decided we need money.

But we were not just deciding we need money. We were deciding that we are the need to have money. Talk about leaving ourselves extra powerless! From this moment, our identity included the thought and experience of always needing more money. Now, no matter how much money we have, we will still have this feeling of needing more.

Did we need more money? Did we need to see ourselves as the ongoing need for money? No. The deeper Truth is to realize that it was not money we were seeking; it was not money we were needing. We simply needed to stop feeling powerless.

And where did this feeling come from? It came from looking up to those with power, such as our parents, believing that we needed what they had. We decided that we were missing something, and if we were more like them, we would be more okay. In simple terms, we decided that we were without what we needed. Then we became the thought 'I am without what I need'.

The Truth is, while we were adding more and more ideas to ourselves, we were feeling more and more without what we needed. Just the idea of needing more ideas left us feeling without, as it was incorrect from the start. It was more accurate and truthful to see that it was not more ideas we needed, but the trust that no extra ideas could make us feel more whole—just emptier.

We have spent our entire lives looking for perfect idea that describes us. We have even been putting all our current ideas to the test trying to prove and validate that they absolutely and wholly describe who we are. What we have avoided looking at is that there is not an idea that aptly describes us—least of all the ideas we have accumulated along the way, no matter how uplifting or empowering they may seem, and no matter how far they have gotten us thus far.

Nothing we think about ourselves will do because no thoughts describe what we are. We once thought they could, but they fall short every time. We are not the same substance of a thought. The word 'who' has described the I, but as we clearly are not the I, we are therefore not a 'who'. Now you can see that we are certainly not the need for more money; that is the void.

So what are we really? We are that which provides, not that which needs. The trick is to start seeing yourself as that which receives infinitely, as well as that which provides infinitely. Achieving that is your Enlightenment.

We are the infinite that provides infinitely and keeps receiving infinitely.

I do not want to be here anymore

If you have ever gone through dark times in your life and experienced wanting to exit the Earth, there are a cluster of beliefs responsible for this. They include thoughts like 'I do not want to live'; 'I do not want to exist anymore'; 'I do not want to be me any longer'; 'I do not want this body anymore'; 'I do not belong here'; 'People do not want me here'; and 'I want to cancel myself out'. If you have ever wondered what thought is behind creating cancer, look at the above list and see which thought it might be.

At this point, it is important to mention that illness and the thoughts we have been discussing are one and the same. There is no delineation between the two. Illness is the effect a thought has on the body; illness is how a thought presents itself in the body.

Many experts have been scratching their heads for years trying to understand how to heal illness. The reason the answers have been so elusive is that the answers are not found in the body, but rather in the Mind. Our thoughts are the illness, and if you want to heal the body, you must heal the Mind. It is a good thing that is exactly what we are doing right now.

For every thought and belief, there is a unique symptom in the body. This means that behind every illness there is a very specific thought or cluster of thoughts. The Mind stores different beliefs in different parts of the body, so they have very specific effects on specific areas. In my previous book—*The All Knowing Diary*—I go into more detail on this subject.

To give you a general introduction, thoughts are stored in the parts of the body that relate to that thought. For example, thoughts to do with intimate relationships and our fears around that, generally appear within our reproductive organs and can affect how well we can conceive a child. Specifically for a woman, thoughts around being a great mother often appear in the breasts. Thoughts about our inability to move forward or our need to keep moving appear around our hips, legs, ankles, and feet.

It is not a coincidence that specific parts of the body show up as specific type of thoughts. In fact, that is the design of the body; it is based on giving

you specific experiences. The quality of those experiences gets reflected in those parts of the body. The better the quality of experience you are having, the better the quality of health you will experience in those body parts. Higher-frequency thoughts create healthier body parts.

With that in Mind, it is very important that we deal with these nasty beliefs above. You can imagine what impact a thought such as not wanting to be here anymore has on our body? People say that we start dying from the time we are born. And in a lot of cases this is correct. Not because that is the design of the body, but because we have beliefs that cancel out life.

As I said, every belief takes its toll in some way or another. Some might cause commitment phobias, some might cause reproductive issues, some might cause deterioration in your eyesight, and some will cause death. I call these 'thoughts that kill'.

I am not trying to scare you, because with the power of awareness, we can reverse these effects and get the body healed again. And that is exactly what we are doing right now—we are harnessing our heightened awareness to see what lies beneath the surface of the Mind.

Let us explore the beliefs around not wanting to be here anymore, not belonging here anymore, not liking ourselves being here and feeling that we should be canceled out.

Interestingly, these thoughts are all about themselves. For example, 'I do not want to be here anymore is us not wanting that thought to be here anymore. 'I do not belong here anymore' is not actually about us, but rather about the thought itself that does not belong here anymore. 'I do not like myself being here' is a bit deeper, as it is about the I we have chosen and not wanting to have it around any longer. Again, it is not wanting the I to be here rather than us not wanting to be here.

'I should be canceled out' is particularly interesting because it is about the thought itself that should not exist, and I find it often stems from parents that were considering an abortion but instead conceived. I know this

is controversial, but me telling you this whole time that you as you know yourself does not actually exist is controversial too, so I am running with it.

The point is that we get these beliefs, these thoughts, from someone even as early as in the womb. We are taking it all in from the time of conception until we day we depart. So, it is a good reMinder to new parents to be very careful of what you are thinking about with the new life form growing within you. That new life feels everything!

Yes, we feel thoughts—we all do, and we always have. Thoughts are energy, and we feel them. Knowing you can feel them and knowing what you are feeling is labeled being highly intuitive or psychic. The Truth is that we have been doing this since the beginning.

I will even go a step further. The belief 'I need to cancel myself out' is one of the biggest causes of cancer on the planet. The illness of cancer is us trying to eradicate or cancel ourselves out. People always have a reason for it, but it is not a truthful reason, just a significant one. Despite the reasons, the thought was planted much earlier on like a seed waiting to grow. It takes a certain experience to water that seed and bring that belief into its full momentum in the Mind and body.

There is another nasty belief here, which is 'I do not want to see myself'. You can imagine what this is doing to your eyesight. This is about not wanting to look at the collection of ideas we have had about ourselves. It is from a point in time when we realized we did not make great choices in assembling our I. Also, seeing what choices others had made caused us to not be very pleased with our own.

Again, this thought is about itself. It does not want to look at itself, nor does it want to look at the I. Herein lies the cause of much suffering. The I is made up of things others do not like, things it does not like, things it does not believe should exist, things it does not want to look at—and worse, it carries no love for itself. So, it can never be what it hopes to be. It is like Pinocchio wanting to be a real boy. The Mind is striving to be seen as real, as lovable, as light itself. But it is none of those things.

Let us go a bit deeper. The belief 'I do not want to be here' is about feeling trapped as this made-up self, the I. We do not want to keep seeing ourselves as this I, and because we feel stuck, we do not want to be here. We feel stuck believing we must be everything we made up about ourselves. It is as if we feel we are committed now, and there is no turning back.

'I am stuck for life' is the belief at play. Once again, this thought is not about us being stuck with anything or anywhere; it is the belief that feels stuck, not us. In Truth we were never stuck, just burdened. It is like accumulating a bunch of debt and not knowing how to become free of it.

Ironically, what has many of us accumulate a lot of debt is our attempt to get away from our beliefs by trying to move in the opposite direction. Buying more, having more, feeling more is what the beliefs push us toward. But it does not work. As I have said before, doing what your beliefs say you should do does not heal them; Truth does.

In this case, it is understanding that we are not the burden of all these beliefs and it is not our burden, for they do not belong to us. But we decided that we do not want them here anymore; we do not want to be them anymore. We do not like ourselves with them anymore. In deciding these things, we created a need to not be them or have them. Needing the beliefs away from us has created another idea stuck about us, causing the beliefs stay even longer.

So what is the Truth? There are two main beliefs tying all of this together: 'I need this to be myself' and 'I need myself'. These are two very strong beliefs tying together two powerful concepts—one of them being to need, and the other being 'myself'. Neither of these statements have any Truth to them. The I is fictitious, needing is the void as it is made up of needs, and 'myself' is a misunderstood concept that is not about us but rather about the I we thought we were.

In Truth, there is no need for 'myself'. It is not a self we ever needed, least of all one made up of needs. 'Myself' is just a thought—or better said, the way that a thought talks about itself. A thought is a self; it has a

self—we do not. And that is where the biggest confusion in human history has come from. We confused a thought having a self with us having a self.

"ME—My Everything—is thought-free, self-free."

It is optional if I am here or not, and it is temporary that I am here

These beliefs are a continuation from the above beliefs that make us not feel very positive about life. They cause depression and definitely stifle motivation in big way.

It is important to realize that we exist no matter what, whether our body is alive or not. The Mind-self does not, but our True Self will always exist. That is the nature of what we are. What is optional is whether we want to align ourselves wholeheartedly with being the I. That is optional.

The question is whether we really want to see this collection of beliefs we have accumulated in this lifetime as our one and only self? The answer is that we never really wanted them as our-self, but rather just to get to know our True Self. We held onto these beliefs and thought that as we can see everything that we are not, we can now see everything that we are.

This method was optional, but we insisted on it. It is not we who are optional; it is how we choose to see ourselves that is optional. Unfortunately, we chose a belief that says how we see ourselves will need to die someday soon, and this was reinforced with the idea that death will bring about a new us to experience. Together these ideas have brought about the death process in some of us much sooner than we would otherwise have experienced it.

The next belief we opted for is that we are not wanted here. Once again, it is the belief saying that about itself. The belief 'I am not wanted here' is not wanted here, but we are treasured here. A lot of this came from trying to squeeze in more ideas about ourselves on top of other ideas, and guess what happened? Those ideas reacted to being near one another inside our body.

One thought argued with the other until many of them pushed a few out, believing that these ideas about ourselves do not represent all of ourselves and so we do not want them around. Sounds crazy, does it not? But ideas are energies unto themselves, taking on the view of what they are about. Where do you think your Identity has come from? It is a collection of other conscious energies creating one entity: I.

The result was another belief coming to the fore, which is: 'I do not belong here'. Funnily enough, this was the whole Mind-self talking about representing you as an eternal being. It was correct—it does not belong in that space. It was not talking about whether you belong or not; it was simply referencing itself saying that it and the collective behind the Mind-self do not belong.

We, of course, hear it as we do not belong and have felt very upset ever since. It really was doing us a favor, but we felt it was about us rather than knowing that our feelings are the I, feeling the beliefs we are still carrying around in this world.

The idea that we could not exist—or worse, should not exist—is preposterous! It is beyond the nature of the Universe to think us up and then for us not to be eternal beings. The body takes a big toll being here by dealing with the I, so you can see why it is temporary. But we are anything but temporary—we are existence itself.

The Universe loves bringing beings like us into existence as an extension of itself. The more ideas it has of itself, the more fulfilling the whole enormous dance really is. You may have noticed a similarity here. We have been adding ideas about ourselves, and the Universe adds ideas about itself. This is quite the profound observation; as the adage goes: 'As above, so below'.

The difference is that we are not meant to add ideas about ourselves, because we are already one of the ideas the Universe has added to itself. Instead, we are meant to explore the idea that we are. This expands our awareness of ourselves, and therefore expands the Universe's awareness of

itself. Adding more ideas to ourselves is simply the slow way; we do eventually figure out that these ideas are not representative of the being who we truly are. Seeing the type of being we are, is really what this book is all about. We have had to go through seeing very clearly who we are not, and what we are not made up of. So, are you getting closer to understanding your true nature yet? If yes, fantastic—if no, also fantastic!

The ideas we have about ourselves are temporary. The I is temporary. But what is ME is eternal.

I need to know

Together we have looked at many needs so far. But there is one that keeps getting in the way of healing all the other needs. It is the need to know. The reason this is so tricky is that, like all other needs, it comes from the space of being without—in this case being without knowing.

If you inherently believe that you need to know, it is the same as saying that you do not know. You are asserting to yourself that you currently do not have something you think you need. Knowing is seen as essential, as the prerequisite to solving all other problems. This is how it trips us up, because to know the Truth is difficult if we believe that we do not know.

Let us look deeper into this. Firstly, the belief that we do not know is not about us at all. It is not talking about whether we know or do not know. It is the belief believing that it does not know. It was never us without knowing. How can we ever be without knowing when we are the All? The All is All Knowing, as it is everything, which includes all the knowing in the Universe.

Our brain was designed to receive knowing frequencies from the center of the Universe, like a radio receiving sound from the broadcaster. Or better stated, the Universe broadcasts a profound 'Wi-Fi' signal, and that soft, delicate matter called our brain and the organs surrounding it were all purposefully placed there to pick up on what frequencies we need most to excel at our purpose in life.

Our DNA sets the main frequency dial to correspond with the messages we need to pick up on most. DNA is more than just biological matter; it is a frequency of information that is constantly receiving new updates and modifications. It is how we evolve over our lifetime, and it is how other species evolve over time. The center of the Universe knows all; it is the nerve center of an enormous brain that uses galaxies, stars, planets, and yes, even people as its brain tissue.

Our brain is a microcosm of the Universe; it is a scale model. It is ironic, as we have spent lifetimes believing that the Mind is the source of our intelligence. The Universe is the source, and the Mind has been the gatekeeper, scrutinizing what gets allowed in and what does not.

Sometimes you see truly gifted people—musicians, artists, surgeons, sports stars, enlightened teachers—that demonstrate a perfect connection to this infinite knowing, and then there is the rest of humanity whose knowing is being choked by their beliefs.

We are not always aware of the full breadth of our knowing, as it seeps in between the cracks from all our beliefs, needs, and doubts. What makes it harder to receive this information is this belief that we do not know.

This belief originated when we were trying to know whether we needed more information about ourselves than we had. Others were offering us all kinds of ideas. It seemed to be all the rage for people of all walks of life to take on these new ideas of themselves. But we were skeptical. It was this not knowing that led us to believing we are not knowing.

We think that we do not know who we are without these ideas. We saw building a Mind full of ideas and labels as the way to know ourselves, to feel in the know. But you know how the story goes now—the more ideas we took on, the faster we sacrificed knowing for thinking.

Not knowing was never us, but not trusting all those years ago that we were better off without the labels got us into trouble. We believed that we

cannot trust this empty space of quiet and stillness, when everyone else was filling their heads with the noise of knowing who they believed they were.

People did not know who they were; they just knew who they believed they were. Big difference! We were attracted to this quasi-knowing, even if it was lousy and about to ruin lives all around us.

The Truth is that we did not need to make up stuff about ourselves to feel like we knew something or knew ourselves from others. We knew that—we did not trust it, but we knew that. We had knowing, but we did not recognize it for what it was in the moment.

We know not to believe what is in the Mind, even if everyone else is believing it.

I am poor

One of the ways we know that these subconscious beliefs are there is when they get triggered. When we relive a similar experience to the one that had us decide on a belief, we feel it coming up and taking over our senses. We call this a RE-action. It is where we are RE-acting out an experience from our past.

The belief 'I am poor' can be felt as feeling poor when you cannot afford or should not afford a particular experience. You might walk into a luxury hotel, an expensive car dealer, or a fancy restaurant and immediately feel poor. We have often mistaken these feelings as being who we are because this is how we are feeling about ourselves. But this is not what is going on at all.

You are not having a feeling about who you are; rather, your awareness has picked up on what you decided to believe about yourself many years ago, and you are feeling that belief again. Beliefs feel to us like what they describe.

Your awareness is always trying to heal the past by showing up what you still believe that is not the Truth. We feel what our beliefs feel like, and

we think that this is who we are, and we get upset because we think it is the Truth about us. However, our feelings are not representative of who we are, because we are simply feeling who we are not.

In this case, a long time ago, we decided to believe that we are poor, and it stuck like the other decisions we made about ourselves. It gets re-experienced whenever this belief is triggered.

So what is the Truth? Firstly, the belief 'I am poor' is a poor belief. It is not describing who we are; it is describing itself. Furthermore, it was a poor choice to represent ourselves, as it left us feeling that we have less than others; and we have less than we need. It also describes the beliefs those around us had taken on and insisted were the Truth. Ultimately, it was a poor choice for us and them, but we were never poor.

What really made us feel poor was selling out on our greatness by taking on more beliefs just to fit in. We saw others around us feeling bad about themselves, and we believed that we must follow suit to be accepted. This really hurt us.

We had hoped that taking on more beliefs and ideas of ourselves would cause us to feel more. But it has just made us feel less. The idea that we need more to be more is a poor idea. We never needed ideas to feel rich; that is just a poor man's game.

We can see ourselves as rich, without having more or needing more. That is a rich person's game! Needing less, and seeing ourselves as more leads to great abundance in all areas of life.

I am afraid of my life

Some of us had a wonderful upbringing and welcomed each day with joy and excitement. But some of us had a rocky start and even a rocky adulthood, and we now begin each day with little dread, anxiety, and fear of what the day will bring. That is largely to do with deciding on beliefs like this one and similar beliefs, such as 'I cannot trust life to look after me'; 'Life hurts'; and so on.

The fear that we feel is what this belief feels like. We are fearing fear itself. Remember that every belief has a feeling based on what it is describing or what it is all about. So, 'I am afraid of my life' feels inside of us like fear to do with our life. We are not afraid of life or what is to come; it is just having this belief inside of us that creates those feelings. Knowing this helps us delineate the Truth, which is how we feel about our life versus feeling what it feels like to have this belief stuck in our Mind and body.

So, what is the Truth? Every time we came to add a new belief or idea about ourselves, we experienced a bit of dread, anxiety, and fear. We became worried about what we were going to hit ourselves with next. It was not life we were worried about, but rather ourselves.

We learned to worry about how much harder we were going to make our lives each day. And now we relive the worry and anxiety; this time it is based on not adding new beliefs but on what we will do to try and compensate for the ones we picked.

Remember, the Mind has us think that the way to heal the feelings and the pain caused by a belief is to compensate for it. The Mind says that if you feel like you are unloved, go out there and draw attention to yourself. If you feel unrecognized in the world, go be impressive. If you feel like you are a failure, push yourself to achieve something incredible.

The Mind is constantly leading us around by the nose, having us cross rivers, climb mountains, and take from ourselves and our environment just to feel better about ourselves. It never says to just get to the Truth about how we are feeling—that would be the short and smart path.

It is listening to the Mind that now causes us to be afraid of our life. We wonder what it will make us do today, what it will have us upset at ourselves for today. The Mind has a go at us every day, making life harder than it needs to be.

What we are really upset about is even deeper. It is that we have listened to the Mind our entire life, and we are worried that today we will listen to it all over again. It is not life we fear; it is our very own Mind.

We intrinsically fear that we will listen to it again and again, and worst of all, believe it again and again. In Truth we are worried that we will believe what our Mind says about us and tells us to do, to be happy. This creates fear because it causes us to believe we cannot just be happy the way we are.

The hidden belief is that we must believe our Mind or believe what we think. Years ago, we committed to believing what we think. This is very scary for us because we do not know what we will think next.

The Truth is that 'I must believe myself or my Mind' is the belief talking about itself. We do not have to believe our Mind because we are not the thought thinking that. It says it must believe what its Mind or I says. We do not because we do not have one, so what is there to believe in or listen to?

It is not our Mind; it is the I of all the thoughts trapped inside making us stuff up all the time. We can eavesdrop, but these are not conversations that relate to us in any way. The noise all these thoughts make, just shows us what we still think is us that is not. Believing something is us that is not, is quite scary.

'I am scared' is once again the thought thinking that for itself. It is what is scared.

Now that you know this, you have nothing left to be afraid of.

I hate everything I do and everything I create

Does it ever feel like whatever you do is never good enough, never quite as perfect as you hoped it would be? Does the thought that someone else would have done it better haunt you?

There is a very nasty belief we have not quite dealt with yet, that we must hate everything we do. There is hatred in many of us, and even though we hate to admit it, it is there. Hatred is not something that is ever about us. We think it is, we feel it is, and it is easily the most horrible feeling in the human experience. After all, it is the opposite of love.

This hatred comes from trying to draw on some form of power when we were growing up. Many of us felt helpless in our family or schooling situations. Hatred was one of the only forms of power available to us. What we did not realize was that it was power against us, not power for us.

When we decided to call upon this power, we felt hatred toward ourselves for having brought this type of thought into our lives. And so began the idea to hate whatever we do. The thought behind this was that if we have to bring hate into our lives, how can we truly love what we are or what we do in life? We resented ourselves for inviting hatred in, and this began the hatred toward ourselves.

The thought: 'I hate myself for that' lingers in the background and is, of course, a very toxic thought to be carrying around. The idea that 'I can hate what I create' is also very toxic because it comes from an originating thought 'I hate that I ever existed'.

Before you take this too personally or too seriously, recognize that it is all about the I ever existing. Many of us came to think that we hate that we ever created the I. We hate having ever believed that we were this I that was created. We hate that we ever gave it so much power over us, assigning our whole identity to it. It was never us in the first place, yet we have spent years believing it is the sum-total of who we are. We hate this about ourselves.

So, what is the Truth? If we look at 'I hate', we can see it is the I that hates. Furthermore, we can see that I hate is the thought I hate describing what it does, how it thinks, and how it exists. It is a thought, like all the others, having a thought about itself and what it does. It was never about us or what we do. So, we do not need to hate what we have done in the past, because having the thought of hate never came from us in the first place.

Thoughts are borrowed because they already exist in the Universe. We do not own them; we do not birth them; we just choose to experience them until we do not. It is like breathing oxygen. We do not own the air

we breathe; we did not birth it, so to speak, but we draw upon it and experience it.

There is nothing to hate inside of us, because the I was never us in the first place, and the hatred was the I hating itself, not us hating it. We just confused its hatred for our own.

The thought 'I hate what I make' is once again the I hating what it makes. It is the thought 'I hate what I make' talking about itself.

These thoughts give us contrast in our experience of being alive. They show us who we are not and what we are not, which helps us return to who and what we truly are.

We are not the hatred of all things, but rather the love for all things.

We can love that we brought in an I to show the many facets of human experience.

We can love the I for being there to show us the Truth about ourselves—that "I" was never the I in the first place.

What a relief that is!

I am going to get it wrong

Getting something wrong in life, or even getting life wrong, is one of our biggest fears. But what are we really fearing? Is it not seeing ourselves for who we really are? Is it making a mistake about ourselves and making decisions believing we are one way, when we are anything but who we believe we are? The biggest mistake we can make in life is not recognizing ourselves correctly.

Mistakes, if there truly is such a thing as a mistake, can only come from deciding in a non-truthful space. When you are being self-loving, seeing yourself correctly, you cannot make a mistake. If on the other hand, you are needing to prove yourself to the world or impress someone, if you are coming from a space of self-doubt and neediness, then the decisions born from this space will create very undesirable outcomes, ending in an amplified experience of self-doubt and neediness.

The mistake is in the space, not in the decision or outcome. Likewise, success is right at the start, also in the space, and so what follows will be a successful outcome. Success or failure is not the gamble it may seem; it occurs right at the start. The mistake is to not see ourselves as a success. Getting it right, getting life right, begins by seeing ourselves correctly.

Where did this notion of making a mistake even come from? It began with the thought that we need a self—an I. The moment we decided to add to ourselves was when we first felt like we made a mistake. This continued time and time again as we added new beliefs, one on top of another. No matter how good our selection was, they were still only beliefs, not Truths, so the feeling of having made a mistake continued.

We felt we got it wrong by needing an I; we felt we got it wrong for having an I. We got it wrong by trying to add more beliefs in attempt to make having an I right again. Continuing to justify and prove the validity of the I we chose is also the source of experiencing further mistakes in life.

The belief that we made a mistake is like all other thoughts. It is not us talking; it is itself talking. We just used this thought to feel what making a mistake feels like, and to feel what having a mistaken I feels like. Remember, thoughts are tools to experience different feelings, but no matter how strong or real they feel, they are not us. They are not our substance.

Believing that we are the mistake, is the mistake. Believing that I am the I, in the thought 'I am the mistake' was also a mistake. When we heard and felt the thought 'I am the mistake', we actually thought we needed to be the I to have it fit. The thought 'I need an I' was behind this.

But it is only the thoughts that need an I—that is their intended makeup. So, it is true for a thought to think and believe that it needs an I and must have an I. Those are correct statements. It was all about them, but never about us. The thought 'I need an I' was the thought acknowledging that to itself.

Going even deeper, however, it is important to look at that thought I. There is a lot of identifying with what is not there. The thought I is also a thought about itself, about the originating thought behind the thoughts themselves. They all began with this one single foundation. Without the I, no other thoughts could exist. The I is what gives them their self.

So how do we say I without it being in reference to our Identity in any way, shape, or form?

Realize that I—or I am, if it helps—is the full body of all thoughts talking about all of itself. There are billions and trillions of various thoughts scattered throughout the Universe, and they refer to themselves as the I or I am. But do not be confused, because even though this collective is enormous, there is far more beyond them.

This is where you come into it. We are that which exists beyond thoughts, beyond the I singularly or as a collective I. It is time to see that. I is the thoughts talking about themselves. I am is also all the thoughts talking about themselves, but it goes further to say that they are whatever they say about themselves. They are how they define themselves.

I is not our idea of our-Self and never was. We took our idea of our-Self from the idea thoughts had about themselves. We borrowed it. It is time to let it go. It happens to all of us time and time again.

To experience and feel our enormity is the path for us now. We are done being and experiencing thoughts, so now let us recognize that I am is the thought I am referring to itself. Of course, there is a huge attachment to this particular thought.

The way to let it go is to realize that I am refers to the collective all thoughts still trapped within our body's subconscious Mind. But we do not identify with the food trapped between our teeth, so let us not identify with thoughts trapped in our body either.

The way to do this is to see that they are all part of the much greater I am collection of thoughts, but we are separate from that. We are feeling what it feels like, but it is not us.

"ME—My Everything—is the idea of myself that has not been thought of so far. I am an idea, so whole and complete, that it never needed any new thoughts about itself."

My ideas are not enough

Hopefully by now it has become apparent that everyone of us is so much more than the total accumulation of thoughts we have had about ourselves. When we go beyond the Mind, we can see that we are infinitely more than any one concept or definition. There is, however, an idea that helps point to what we are at our essence. That is the term idea—that we are a unique idea, thought of by the Universe.

An idea is a being. Like a thought, it is the very essence of what that idea is about. Imagine that for everybody walking around, there is an idea inhabiting that body. Sometimes, if an idea is so important on the Earth, it will inhabit many bodies at the same time. So, when we refer to our True Self, what we are referring to is the infinite idea that we are. As an idea, we are eternal, never-ending, only evolving.

There are many ideas on Earth, and the clearer you become on what idea you are, the happier you will be. Some are the idea of Truth, some are the idea of compassion, some are the idea of electricity, some are the idea of healing, some are the idea of music, etc. We all come together in bodies to make life on Earth as amazing as possible. Those who embrace their idea excel not only in their own life, but also make a real difference to the rest of us too.

What idea are you?

One of the greatest gifts we can give to ourselves in our lifetime is to recognize what idea we are. This is where self-love comes from. When we move away from all the thoughts and ideas we previously had about ourselves, to recognizing the idea we truly are, it becomes very easy to be in love with ourselves. In fact, our body has been designed to bring our idea to the world. The more we love and express our idea, the healthier our bodies become. The less we express our idea, the more our bodies suffer.

You can think of this in terms of life purpose. All things have a purpose—from the spider that catches insects, the bees that pollinate flowers, and the trees that make oxygen and create homes, everything is on purpose. We, too, have a purpose; our idea is that purpose.

To live our idea is nature's success guarantee. To be on purpose means to celebrate all that we are, without comparison, competition, or self-doubt. A bee does not compare itself to a spider, nor a spider to a bee. A tree does not compare itself to other trees because it knows that when it is focused on being itself, it has the support of the whole Universe behind it. This is why human beings struggle. We decided that our ideas are not enough, or that our idea is not enough.

As we saw all the ideas others were taking on, we decided that we needed new ideas about ourselves. We took on as many as we could find, from the sublime to the ridiculous, from the kind to the cruel; we took them all on and have been compensating for them in life ever since.

To dismiss our own idea as not enough wounded us significantly. It pushed away our true greatness, and we have been searching for it ever since. But what this belief was pointing to is the I. It was trying to help us. It was saying that its ideas were never going to be enough for us. It was not that our ideas were never going to be enough, and it was not about our idea of our True Self.

It was about all the ideas it was going to have that were never going to be enough. And it was true! The Mind has ideas, but they take more from us than they give. Look around the planet to see what ideas have come from the Mind; you will see that they take more than they give. Our idea-Self—our True Self—also has ideas, which we experience as inspiration or *Intuition Wisdom.*

The I knew that what it had to offer would never be enough, would never come close to what we already have within us. The idea that we are is infinite; the ideas of the Mind are finite. Here the I is also saying that its ideas of itself are not enough, and it is true because its idea of itself does

not come close to the idea that we are. The idea of a self would never come close, and that is the point. Trying to maintain a self—an Identity—is what has made us feel that we were never enough, because an I was never our Truth.

Hidden within this belief that our ideas are not enough is also another belief, that we are not worth loving as the idea that we are. Since believing that thought, we have been looking for that love in all the wrong places. We have searched high and low, looking everywhere but where it exists—not outside of us, but inside of us. We are exactly what is worth loving.

Here, again, the thought was talking about itself and how it sees itself as not worth loving. It was never about us. The more ideas we took on, the more we felt this was real and about us. In Truth, the more of our own idea we take on, the more we experience feeling loved. We are an idea coming from love.

A version of the belief that our ideas of ourselves are not enough is also hiding in the background. We felt that we got our ideas of ourselves wrong. That we are wrong, that the ideas are wrong, and so it loops around and around. The Truth is that the I got its ideas of itself wrong, not us. It was talking about itself.

In Truth we never got to see what our own ideas really were before taking on new ones. We never gave ourselves enough of a chance to explore our own ideas, to explore all that we truly are.

This brings us to another belief lurking in the background—a very unique belief, as it is both Truth and belief all at once—that we never needed thoughts in the first place. It is not a Truth about us per se, as we are not an I. It is rather a Truth about itself. What is being said here is that 'I never needed thoughts, which is the I that represents the sum total of all thoughts coming to a realization about itself. That is, the I never needed to exist.

This also underpins our deepest Truth, which is that thoughts are never going to fulfill us, never going to point the way to discovering our true nature as infinite beings. Thoughts and the I belong together, but the

I never belonged to us. Thoughts never belonged to us—how can they since they never came from us in the first place? Furthermore, the I never belonged to us, as we never needed thoughts to become something special.

We just needed to see that the idea that we truly are, is like nothing else in the whole Universe.

I do not believe in myself

One of the most important traits in life is self-belief. It is the fuel for greatness, and the magic that creates miracles. Yet so few experience it in their lives. Those who have it shine bright, exhibiting incredible ability in whatever area of life they possess it.

How do we acquire it, or experience it when we have the belief that we do not believe in ourselves?

The trick is to notice in this statement who has no self-belief. Is it really us that is without self-belief, or is it the I? You guessed it! 'I do not believe in myself'—It is the I asserting it has no self-belief. We are not without self-belief.

This belief is all about the Identity that cannot believe in itself. What can the identity believe in when it is made up of one belief after the other? The I is simply made-up.

It is the thought 'I do not believe in myself' that does not believe in itself. Remember, we are neither the I, nor are we the thought 'I do not believe in myself'. We took on this thought, believed it was us, and experienced its meaning ever since. So, when we feel that we cannot believe in ourselves, we are not feeling the lack of belief in us; instead, we are feeling what it feels like to have the thought 'I do not believe in myself' trapped in our Mind and body. But it was never us in the first place. What we feel is this thought thinking about itself.

This began when we believed that our Self—our I—was not going to be enough in this lifetime. We decided to believe in making up a new

self—a new Identity—as the best way forward. And we have been trying to believe in this I, this false self ever since. We did not believe in us, and we did not believe in our True Self and this has upset us ever since it happened all those years ago.

We gave up on our True Self before it had the time to strut its stuff. That is when the I could sneak in the belief 'I do not believe in myself'.

Interestingly, there is a double whammy present. Not only is the I referring to itself, but it is also referring to our True Self, or 'myself'. It is does not believe in a self other than itself. In other words, it does not believe in us. This is where things got challenging. The I is making a point that it does not believe that the true and real part of us—the True Self—exists.

When we identified with the I, we also took on its beliefs as our own. We took on the concept of not believing in the part of us that is Truth. We discarded it and failed to acknowledge it in our lives.

The missing Truth to realize is that we do not need to believe what the I believes. It believes 'I do not believe in myself', so if we are not the I and we do not believe what it believes, this immediately takes out of the equation that there ever was a self—an Identity—that we needed to believe in.

So, what remains is simply love—love for the being we truly are and have always been.

We have always believed in being a being. We have always believed in Love. What we struggled to believe in was being an I. To believe in Love is to believe in your-self as Love-Being.

LOVE BEING is ME.

I am alive

It is hard to argue this belief, and it may be even harder to see how this belief is holding you back. In Truth, this one belief brings about serious illness and dysfunction in the body. How? Let us explore. Understand that it is not you saying you are alive; it is the I.

The I wants to see itself as the body. This would not be a problem except that we took on this thought as if it were our own. In other words, we identified with it. We became the I that is alive. By identifying with this thought, we brought the Mind into the body. If we are now the Mind, and the Mind is now alive through the body, then the body and Mind become intertwined. Many of the thoughts in the Mind harm the body—some worse than others.

It is not we who are alive at all. It is the body that is alive; we are not. We are not the body nor the Mind. The body exists, we exist, but the Mind is made-up, so we certainly do not want a made-up Mind nesting permanently in the body. But even if the Mind is made-up, we still believe it is real. While we believe something is real, it is. And because we believe it is real, it continues to harm the body.

It is the thought 'I am alive' that thinks it is alive, not us. We are not this thought, so we are not what is alive. We decided to be this thought and identify with it many years ago. We also decided that it is one of the most empowering thoughts we could ever have. And we say it with such pride, do we not? We even think to be alive is so precious—and it is, more than we have ever known. Yet it does not change the fact that it is not us that are alive.

It is important to see that in deciding this, we came to believe that the Mind is alive, and with that comes seeing it as one and the same as us. It thinks, but it is not alive. In believing it is alive, we decided something huge, and that is that we birthed the Mind into existence. But we did not. The Mind was something we inherited and then added to. The Mind never needed to be alive, and thinking it is alive causes us to become even more attached to its existence.

Instead, we do not need to see ourselves as this body for it to live. The body lives far better without the Mind interfering with its optimal functioning.

Being alive did not require having a Mind to survive. And we never needed to be alive to exist as ME.

I exist

We are aware of thoughts but we do not think them. We have always felt thoughts around us, and so we have always felt the I all around us.

Despite it being very convincing, very real, and feeling very much all about us, it was never about us. We were never the I energy. It exists, but we do not exist as it.

The I exists separately from us until we decide we want to believe that is who we are. We can love that we have been the I all this time. It has given us many great and wonderful experiences—and many tough times as well. It has certainly showed us who we are and who we are not.

We have felt it all around us, thinking it was us. But feeling is what we do. We do not have thoughts; we feel them. It is our nature to feel; we are feeling beings. We feel thoughts within us; we feel thoughts all around us. We feel other people's thoughts all the time, and we have since birth.

The loudest of all are the thoughts we identified with, calling them our own. We feel these thoughts the strongest. Feeling these thoughts causes a reaction, and this reaction is called emotion. We often think we are reacting to what we are, who we are, and who we will be forever.

But what we experience as feelings are what thoughts feel like in our body. Thoughts trapped in our body feel sad, depressed, excited, hopeless, hopeful, frustrating, annoyed, or angry. How we relate to these thoughts contained within our body gives us our emotions. We have always believed we are reacting to what is real, but we are reacting to what we believe is real.

That is the sneaky thing about thoughts. They feel real and as though they belong to us, as though we are the ones birthing them. But we are not and never were. They already exist, surrounding us all day, every day.

The funny thing is we always believed that to have thoughts is a way to define us as an intelligent species. But believing we are these things called thoughts has diminished our intelligence in immeasurable ways. As an idea, we have limitless intelligence, and always have. What has prevented

that intelligence from surfacing is believing that we are our thoughts, that we are our identity, instead of believing that we are an idea. Ironically, our thoughts limit our intelligence rather than increase it.

Thoughts keep humanity small. They keep us trapped in an alternate reality that continues a pattern of suffering and struggle. Thoughts confuse the brain—they choke it up, one could say—when the intention behind the human brain was to harness anything but thoughts.

A far greater intelligence than the Mind has been available to us this whole time. Our brain functions best when we focus our awareness on the idea that we are. This connects us to limitless inspiration from within. This is our link to the Universe as a whole. As an enormous brain, it is a limitless library of profound knowing. The Universe is full of ideas, some taking the form of a planet, some a galaxy, some stars, some a bee, tree, flower, black hole, or person.

All ideas came from one enormous infinite Circle called love. Love is what we are. Love experiences itself as so many different ideas across so many people—as so many things in so many ways. But if you see life through the lens of the Mind, you never see the Universe this way. The Mind distorts how we see ourselves, so it distorts how we see everything! The Universe, life, and we ourselves are all so much more magical than we have been able to see—until now.

The Universe is conscious, and when it births new ideas, they, too, are conscious. We are these conscious ideas experiencing life in many forms all at once. We can continue to see ourselves as people, or we can see ourselves as so much more. After all, if you want more in life, you must see yourself as more. It is time to be the ideas we came here to be. This will bring harmony and balance to our lives and to the Earth.

So, what is the Truth about the I?

It can be seen as an idea you never needed to have about yourself.

Conclusion

Congratulations you have discovered one of humanity's biggest and most Enlightening secrets. We are NOT the MIND and You are Not an I.

Who thought Enlightenment could be, well, so enlightening, and Losing Your Mind would be so uplifting?

You have just taken a ride all the way back to the first thought, to the very decision that has defined you your whole life.

It has been an incredible journey so far, and I thank you for sharing it with me!

Learning to see yourself as you truly are, signifies a deep awakening that will change all areas of your life. New experiences will open up, new possibilities will come in, relationships all around you will improve, and your intuition wisdom will take quantum leaps.

Most of all, your relationship with yourself will deepen. Having a deep and meaningful relationship with our True Self—My Everything—is what we have all been striving for without even realizing it. It sets the foundation for a great life, transforming our mental well-being and our physical health, and it puts us firmly on our life purpose path. It is the source of financial flow and immense fulfillment.

So, what have we learned on our Losing Your Mind journey, let's recap…

A Mind full of non-truths creates a life full of non-truth. The Mind is a void, and this void creates insatiable needs within us all.

We experience a lot of OVERS in life, over consuming on this Earth, over-taking, always needing more, simply because we have a lot of UNDERS in life: under-nurturing, under-appreciating, and under-loving ourselves.

These OVERS are coming from these UNDERS. What we refuse to give to ourselves, we make up for by taking more from all that is around us.

We discovered that there are many insane beliefs in the Mind causing these UNDERS and OVERS. These subconscious beliefs control our lives and create our life experiences from inside of us. They dictate our needs, our thoughts, our decisions and our actions, affecting the quality of our entire lives. Why? Because we believe they are true.

We learned the Mind is a void and how to fill this void. It's not by doing what it says or giving it what it needs but by looking at the Truth.

We are learning that the MIND has been storing virtually every negative, self- loathing thought, belief, idea, disappointment and rejection inside our body! This causes ageing and is responsible for the many "incurable" diseases humanity battles with every day. The body reflects the Mind, so to heal the body we must often heal the Mind first. In fact, life is reflecting the Mind everywhere you look. The Mind creates pain and suffering, taking more than it gives, promising more than it delivers.

The solution for all of this is: 'Losing Your Mind' or otherwise referred to as Evolution. This is the experience of reaching a point in life without needing beliefs or concepts about everything. In fact, it is about being in life without the need for a self-concept—your current identity, the person you believe you are. This is true freedom, and the ultimate definition of success.

We discovered the Mind loves to label and define everything, because it is made up and is trying to make itself out to be real.

The Mind has thoughts, but they are not our true nature, nor do they come close to describing our true nature. We can experience thoughts and what they feel like, but we are not thoughts.

What we are—our true nature—cannot be described or defined. We experience what we believe about ourselves. The more we see, believe and imagine ourselves to be, the more we get to experience in life.

We learned that whatever we identify with, we become it and experience it. To date, we chose to identify with the Mind-self and its thoughts, so that has been our experience in life. As we are innately formless beings occupying a body, we can choose to see ourselves and identify with anything. So, why not go for the biggest thing we know – the Universe. When we identify with the universe we return home, back to our true-self, an infinite Love-being.

The Mind is not who we are, nor what we have come to think of it. It is a thinking, needing 'I' unto itself. We choose whether to place our awareness on the 'I' to experience the void, or whether to place our awareness on our Idea-Self—our True Self—to experience our wholeness and completeness.

We can easily and effortlessly return to a Mindless space by being in Truth in nature or with the help of the EnlightenMe Machine.

I'd like to share a wonderful little mantra I use to help me elevate into a truth space. "I Seek Truth And Wisdom, Not The Mind. Please Leave Me In A Space Of Stillness"

I say this to myself repeating it at least three times.

We learned that the Mind has many needs it wants us to fulfill for it. But its needs are not our needs and so pursuing its needs will not bring fulfillment, just more emptiness. It has created goals and ambitions for itself such as needing to be a someone, needing to get somewhere in life, needing attention, needing to be noticed and respected by others. Its needs send us up the garden path, looking for love in all the wrong places – always outside of ourselves.

We discovered that we are the ones worthy of our own attention, and the more we give it to ourselves, the more loved, noticed, and recognized we feel. We have realized that there is no need to compare ourselves or compete with others because what we are is so extraordinary and so unique that the Universe went to extraordinary effort to bring us into existence, or we wouldn't be here. It was only the 'I' that was the same as the other 'I's, and

'I's love to compare and compete. "I's" never feel enough because they are made up!

We realized that the Self we have been aware of, is the Mind's Self not our Self. Thoughts have a "self" we DO NOT! The accumulation of all the thoughts-self has created the experience of us having a self.

Best of all, when we go beyond the Mind we have our truth, infinite and loving, our connection to the 'knowing' of the Universe. Each of us have so much to explore inside this being, we could spend every day learning, as I have, and we would need infinite lifetimes to even scratch the surface.

To sum up the highlights, here is a quick recap:

- The Mind is full of BeLIEfs.
- These BeLIEfs create our reality.
- BeLIEfs dictate how we feel, what we need, what we do, and how we see ourselves and our life.
- A BeLIEf is a thought—a thought about itself.
- Thoughts have a feel based on what they describe.
- Thoughts also have a Self—an 'I'—but we do not.
- We chose to add new thoughts to ourselves, believing this would add to our life.
- All this added was an 'I'—a Mind-Self.
- We believed that this was our 'self', but it was the thought-self.
- The more thoughts we added, the less we felt our True 'Self' and the worse we felt.
- Our True Self is love, and the further we disconnect from this, the more pain we experience.
- We attempt to heal this pain by adding to ourselves, doing more, having more, trying to be more.
- This just ends badly for everyone.

- Instead of adding thoughts to ourselves, we needed to take away our thoughts about ourselves.
- Truth is the healing we have been looking for.
- When we feel poorly, we are feeling the thoughts still trapped within our body.
- Trapped thoughts harm and age the body, causing all kinds of illness and disease.
- There are literally thousands of harmful thoughts still trapped in our body causing pain, suffering, emotional instability and throwing us off track in our lives
- It's important to make time to rid our body of all the trapped thoughts stuck in our cells. The EnlightenMe Machine is designed specifically for this task.
- The less thoughts trapped in our body the healthier and more intuitive we become.
- The Mind is not the source of our greatness, but rather the hindrance to it.
- Beyond the Mind lies a far greater intelligence, the Universe's Intelligence, speaking through our intuition and inspiration.
- We see this intelligence every day, in our cells, in Mother Nature, in the stars; it is everywhere, everything.
- The Mind disconnects us from this Intelligence.
- We are this intelligence. We always have been and always will be.
- We are the Universe.

Wow! Life Changing!

It is worth sitting and allowing the enormity of this experience to sink in. I hope you loved it as much as I have loved sharing it with you.

You now have the understanding that you are not your thoughts. You understand that how you feel about yourself is not actually how you feel about yourself, but how certain thoughts feel inside of you.

You have learned that emotions are the reactions to having these thoughts left inside of you believing they are true about you. You are neither the thoughts nor the reactions they cause.

When you are aware of a thought, remember it is not about you, it is about itself. Thoughts are a substance, different to us, and they are always describing themselves and never us. If you identify with a thought, you will feel what a thought feels like. As soon as you dis-identify from a thought it stops hurting you.

For example, a thought like "I don't matter" hurts us because we believe we are the 'I' in that sentence. So, we believe it is describing us. We are not the I, the thought has an I, we do not. So, the thought is describing itself.

Let's translate beliefs that we once believed were about us into the truth:

I am all alone

– this is not about you, the thought 'I am alone' is who is alone

I am stuck

– this is not about you, the thought 'I am stuck' is who is stuck

I need more

– this is not about you, the thought 'I need more' is who needs more

I make mistakes

– this is not about you, the thought 'I make mistakes' is who makes mistakes

Thoughts don't describe what you do or who you are they describe what they do and who they are. Thoughts are who, you are not a who. Thoughts

have an I, and the thought itself describes its I, not your I, because you don't have an I.

The I was never about us! I stands for identity, not Me.

These thoughts and the whole identity hurts us because we identify with it, but this is coming to an end. Hopefully now you have a new appreciation for why the body is aging, where countless illnesses originate from, and how important it is to clear our Mind and body of all the thoughts we have been accumulating since being in the womb.

Inner work is NOT optional – if you want to live a long healthy and happy life – please spread this message!

You now have a framework to see the Truth for yourself. Start cultivating an awareness of how you feel inside, what thoughts are creating these feelings, and realize they were never you to begin with, just the "I" referring to itself.

When we began this journey, I said none of your beliefs are true. There is, however, Truth to the beliefs. These beliefs tell the Truth about the 'I'. Every belief describes the 'I' accurately, but none of them come close to describing YOU, because you were never the 'I' in the first place.

When you hear yourself beginning a sentence with 'I' remember you are not talking about the real you, just the 'I'.

You are NOT the 'I' and never were.

You are the All.

Realize:

There is no I in ME.

Next Steps

If you'd like to continue your journey ridding your Mind and Body of a lifetime of trapped thoughts and beliefs then join Daniel for 48 weeks of MIND BLOWING clearing using the EnlightenMe Machine! Your life will never be the same again!

Get your EnlightenMe Machine today at www.EnlightenMe.today

If you would like to explore more amazing Truths, get a copy of Daniel's previous books '*The All Knowing Diary*' and '*Mind Lies and The Truths That Will Set You Free*'. And for those adventurous beings, who want to take their Intuition and Life Purpose to the ultimate level we have profound courses at IntuitionWisdom.com.

If you wish to help others grow and prosper, we offer our Intuitive Practitioner training, which takes you beyond a healer, beyond a life coach, and beyond the Mind to change lives. This training equips you with the very same intuitive abilities that Daniel and Sonja use throughout their videos and sessions.

Remember, trust in your feelings. They show you what the Mind cannot know. They show you how to heal the unhealable, and answer the unanswerable.

When you learn to feel instead of think, you will know what the Universe knows. This is living Beyond the Mind.

PS: Remember to reread this book, and if you have not done so already, order your *EnlightenMe Machine* now so you have it in time for your second read.

Thank you for reading.

Daniel, Sonja and the IntuitionWisdom.com Family.

Other Books By Daniel & Sonja

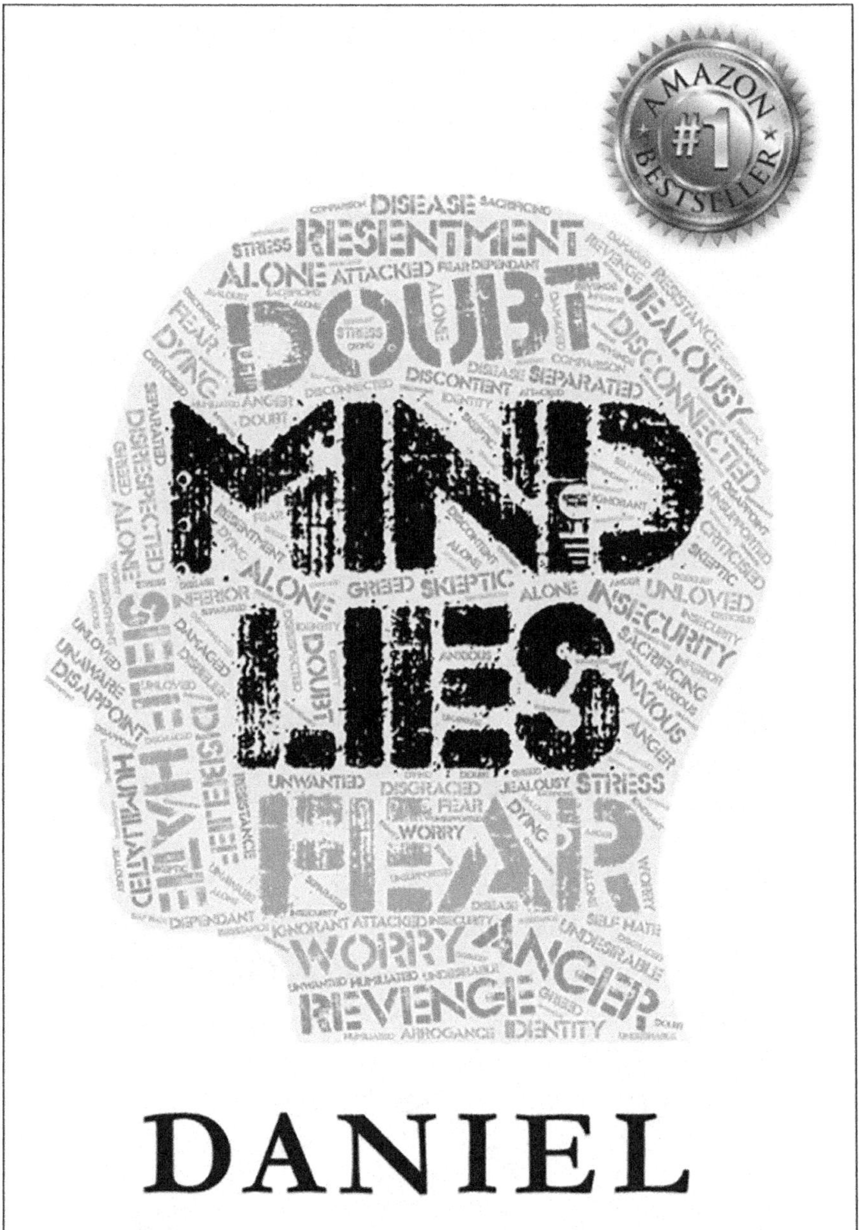
AMAZON
#1
BESTSELLER
DISEASE
RESENTMENT
DOUBT
MIND
LIES
FEAR
WORRY
ANGER?
REVENGE
DANIEL

Natural Pain Free **Birth**

...A Soul's Journey To Earth

Discover The Miracle Of A Soul Conversation With Your Baby

By Sonja & Oliver Rechnitzer

Join our Support Community

We have created a community support program through Facebook.

I recommend that you stay connected and receive ongoing support and gifts along the way!

https://www.facebook.com/groups/intuitionwisdom

Visit us and Subscribe at IntuitionWisdom.com

Thank you for reading.

EVERYTHING THE ‘I’ BELIVES ABOUT ITSELF IS THE TRUTH

It’s Beliefs Were Never Your Beliefs, And They Were Never About You.

Printed in Dunstable, United Kingdom

68521105R00129

Printed in Great Britain
by Amazon

15811778R00031